The Gentle Hook

A Play

Francis Durbridge

A SAMUEL FRENCH ACTING EDITION

SAMUEL FRENCH

FOUNDED 1830

SAMUELFRENCH-LONDON.CO.UK
SAMUELFRENCH.COM

THE GENTLE HOOK

First presented by Bill Freedman and Eddie Kulukundis at the Piccadilly Theatre, London, on the 21st December 1974, with the following cast of characters:

Brad Morris	Raymond Francis
Madge Harrison	Hazel Bainbridge
Alan Kyle	Tony Anholt
Stacey Harrison	Dinah Sheridan
Philip Harrison	Jack Watling
Charles Venner	Brian Moorehead
Lennox	John Quentin
Gerald Waddington	Charles Stapley

The play directed by **Basil Coleman**

Setting by **Hutchinson Scott**

The action takes place in the living-room of Stacey Harrison's ground-floor flat

ACT I	Scene 1	A Wednesday evening in December
	Scene 2	Thursday morning
	Scene 3	Friday morning
ACT II	Scene 1	Friday evening
	Scene 2	Saturday morning
	Scene 3	Saturday night

Time—the present

For the new women in my life . . .
Alexandra, Claire, and Catherine

THE GENTLE HOOK*

ACT I

SCENE 1

The living-room of Stacey Harrison's ground-floor flat near Cadogan Gardens, London. A Wednesday evening—the first week in December

Stacey, a highly successful interior decorator, moved into the flat just over six weeks ago. The living-room reflects her professional good taste. There are two armchairs, a sofa, drinks trolley, record-player, side tables with lamps. The writing-table, with telephone, stands midway between the hall and a high window which occupies practically the whole of one wall. There are several interesting pictures in the room. The entrance hall, which is only partly visible, is reached through an alcove. A door leads to the dining-room and kitchen, and opposite this is an ornate archway leading to the bedrooms and the rest of the apartment (See plan on p. 72)

When the CURTAIN *rises, Brad Morris, Stacey's father, is discovered sitting on the sofa surrounded by presents. There are birthday cards, an LP record, several bottles of after-shave lotion, and a number of art-books on a nearby table. Brad, a retired art teacher, is sixty today.*

As Brad unwraps a package and instinctively shudders at the sight of yet another bottle of after-shave lotion the front-door buzzer is heard. With an impatient shake of the head he puts down the bottle of after-shave lotion and goes out into the hall, to open the front door

Brad (*off*) Why hello, Madge! What a lovely surprise! Come along in.
Madge (*off*) Many happy returns, Brad! You don't look a day over sixty!

Brad enters with Madge Harrison, Stacey's mother-in-law. Madge, a comfortably dressed woman in the late fifties, carries a carrier bag and a gift-wrapped bottle of after-shave lotion

Brad But I am sixty!
Madge Yes, I know. And you don't look it.
Brad (*amused*) But you just said I did!
Madge Did I? Well—happy birthday, anyway! (*She hands him the present*)
Brad (*kissing her*) My dear, you shouldn't!
Madge (*putting down her bag*) I take it that elusive daughter-in-law of mine hasn't returned yet?

---

*N.B. Paragraph 3 on page ii of this Acting Edition regarding photocopying and video-recording should be carefully read.

Brad (*opening the package*) No, she's due back this evening. But you know Stacey. Heaven only knows when she'll arrive! (*He examines the bottle, opens it, and finally sprays a little of the lotion onto his hand*) M'm—M'm! Very, very nice! (*Looking at the label*) "Butch"—I'm flattered.

Madge laughs

Madge What are you doing tonight, Brad, living it up?

Brad As a matter of fact I am. Some ex-pupils of mine are giving a party for me—which in view of the send-off they gave me when I retired is pretty generous of them to say the least.

Madge (*moving to the armchair*) Well, watch it! They'll probably try and talk you into going back. (*She sits*)

Brad The thought had crossed my mind.

Madge (*after a moment*) Have you heard from Stacey?

Brad Yes, she telephoned from Paris early this morning.

Madge Is she well?

Brad Yes, she's fine.

Madge (*after a tiny pause*) Philip's had a letter from her. She definitely wants the divorce.

Brad Did Philip tell you that?

Madge No, but I saw the letter. I looked in on him at his Chambers this morning and it was on his desk. When I asked him about it he said, "For God's sake, Mother, read the bloody thing if you want to!"

Brad Did you read it?

Madge No, of course I didn't! I didn't have to read it! I know my son, Brad. As soon as I saw Philip I knew what had happened.

Brad sits on the arm of the sofa and faces Madge

Brad Madge, why has it suddenly come to a head like this?

Madge I don't think it has suddenly come to a head. They've been having rows, quarrelling, for some time now. If you ask me it started just over a year ago when she met that good looking Swede—whose name I can never pronounce.

Brad (*curiously*) What did you make of that? Was she having an affair with him?

Madge No, of course not! Don't be ridiculous!

Brad They went to Stockholm together, and Philip knew nothing about it until she got back.

Madge But you know your daughter, Brad! She does everything on the spur of the moment. This—what's-his-name—had bought an hotel and he wanted Stacey to do the decor for him. As it happened, she turned down the proposition and told Philip all about it.

Brad After she'd spent three days in Stockholm with what's-his-name.

Madge (*with a shrug*) So what?

Brad (*rising*) Yes, well—I must be honest. I wouldn't have liked it if she'd been my wife. I'd have been as jealous as hell.

Madge Yes, of course—and so was Philip. But Stacey didn't mind that. In fact she'd have been disappointed if he hadn't been jealous. No, what really angered her—what really made her see red—was the fact that he just didn't believe her story.

Brad (*moving to the drinks trolley*) Did she tell you that?

Madge Yes, she did. And she was extremely bitter about it. She said, "I wish now I'd lied to him, Madge. He might have believed me."

Brad Well—we've just got to accept the situation, I'm afraid. There's nothing we can do about it.

Madge I'm not sure Philip's going to accept it. I think he may well put up a fight.

Brad (*picking up a bottle of Scotch*) I hope he does. But if Stacey's made her mind up—if she really does want a divorce—it's all over. (*He looks at the bottle he is holding and is surprised to find it empty*) No wonder I had a hangover this morning! (*Putting the bottle down*) Alan and I must have really gone to Town last night!

Madge Alan Kyle? The young man who works for Stacey?

Brad That's right. He and Stacey are doing the decor for a house just round the corner, in Eaton Place, and since he usually commutes from Dedham Stacey asked him if he'd like to stay here while she was away. I'm glad she did. He makes the best omelettes I've ever tasted. (*Indicating the trolley*) What would you like, Madge?

Madge Nothing for me.

Brad Come along! Just a little one.

Madge No, I won't thank you, darling. (*Rising*) How long have you been staying here, Brad?

Brad Just over a week. I came up for the exhibition at the Hayward and decided to stay on until Stacey got back. I gather Philip's still at the house?

Madge Yes, the Spanish couple are looking after him. Stacey insisted they stayed with Philip. Whether they'll remain with him or not I really don't know.

As Madge speaks we hear the noisy opening and closing of the front door. A moment later Alan Kyle rushes in, attaché case in one hand, evening paper in the other. Alan is in the middle thirties. He has recently sprained his left wrist and is wearing a leather strap on it

Brad Hello, Alan! We were just talking about you!

Alan (*cutting him short; distinctly agitated*) Is Stacey back?

Brad No, not yet.

Alan Oh, God! (*To Madge; in despair*) Hello, Madge. Nice to see you again.

Brad What is it, Alan?

Alan (*throwing his case and newspaper onto sofa*) What a day! What a god-dam, awful, terrible day!

Brad Alan, what's happened?

Alan Everything's happened! Every bloody thing imaginable!

Madge I don't know what you're talking about, but I know exactly how you feel!

Alan Stacey'll go out of her mind when she hears about this afternoon! She'll go raving mad! (*He walks up and down, obviously unable to control his agitation*)

Brad I doubt it. I doubt it very much. But if she does, that'll make two of you. Now take a deep breath, dear boy, and tell us what's happened. Who's murdered who?

Alan (*coming to a standstill*) No-one's been murdered. (*Genuinely relieved*) Thank God! But it was a near thing.

Madge What!

Brad Are you serious?

Alan You bet your sweet life I'm serious! (*Looking at Brad*) It's your friend Peter. He's just been beaten up . . .

Brad (*stunned*) What!

Alan Damn nearly killed.

Brad I—I don't believe it!

Alan It's true, Brad.

Brad Beaten up!

Madge Peter?

Alan Peter Lockwood.

Madge Has a wonderful art collection . . .?

Alan That's right. About six months ago he bought a house in Eaton Place and because Brad was a friend of his he asked Stacey to do it up for him. We've been working on it since June. We finished just before Stacey went away and last Friday I helped Peter to move in. Well—this afternoon someone broke in there, locked the housekeeper in the loo, gagged the cook, and damn nearly clobbered the living daylight out of poor old Peter.

Brad (*still obviously shaken by the news*) Why—it's unbelievable!

Madge Dreadful!

Alan He's in the London Clinic. I've just come from there. They say the poor darling will be all right in a day or two—but my God, it was a nasty experience! (*Pacing up and down again*) And the house! You've never seen anything like it. They must have been through it with a bulldozer. Curtains torn, carpets ripped up, upholstery in shreds!

Brad Jeez!

Alan It's fantastic, Brad. It really is. (*Shaking his head; with a note of desperation*) And apart from anything else—apart from poor old Peter— just imagine how I feel! Six months' work utterly and completely ruined by the bastards!

Brad What did they take, do you know?

Alan I don't know! No-one seems to know.

Madge How did they get in, through one of the windows?

Alan The police seem to think they had a key. According to the housekeeper the telephone rang at about ten minutes to three and for some reason or other no-one answered it.

Madge (*knowingly*) So they thought the house was empty?

Alan Exactly. But the call could have been a perfectly genuine one, of course, or a wrong number for that matter.

Madge This is a dreadful area for this sort of thing. It really is. There's been three burglaries in Cadogan Gardens in the past fortnight.
Brad It can happen anywhere.
Madge Yes, I suppose so. But if you ask me, this town gets more like New York every day! (*She kisses Brad*) Try and enjoy yourself tonight, Brad. (*Moving to the hall*) And tell that daughter-in-law of mine to give me a ring. I'd like to talk to her.
Brad (*moving towards the hall*) Yes, of course.
Madge (*to Alan*) Good-bye.
Alan Good-bye, Madge.

Madge exits with Brad

Alan goes to the drinks trolley and helps himself to a large gin and tonic

Brad enters

Alan (*shaking his head*) Wait till Stacey sees what they've done to her lovely curtains!
Brad But why destroy the curtains, for God's sake?
Alan Well, between you and me, there was a wall safe behind the curtains in the dining room. The bastards couldn't find it and when they did find it they couldn't open it, so they went berserk and ransacked the place. At least, that's the theory.
Brad Was anyone else hurt, apart from Peter?
Alan No, not seriously.
Brad Why did they pick on him?
Alan He heard the cook screaming and tried to raise the alarm. One of the men had a gun in his hand so he hit him with it . . .
Brad Oh, God . . .
Alan Apparently Peter went on struggling so the little bastard hit him again. (*Shaking his head*) Madge's right, you know! This town is getting more like New York every day. Look at Piccadilly Circus, you might as well be in Times Square.
Brad It's not as expensive.
Alan Not yet, thank God! I had a letter from an American friend of mine this morning. He says it costs him a fortune every time he parks his car. He took a girl out to dinner the other night and asked the restaurant owner where his parking lot was. The man said "If I had a parking lot would I be running this lousy restaurant?"

Alan laughs at his story, but Brad is looking serious, his thoughts obviously elsewhere

Brad (*suddenly*) Oh, I'm sorry! What was that, Alan?
Alan I said a friend of mine in New York took a girl out to . . . Oh, skip it! (*Looking at his watch*) How are we for time? My word, if you're due there at seven we'd better get a move on.
Brad There's no need for you to run me out to Kingsford. I can easily go by train.

Alan Nonsense! By the time we've got to Waterloo we'll be half-way there.

The front door is heard to open

Stacey (*off; calling from the hall*) Anybody at home?
Brad (*turning towards the hall*) It's Stacey!

Brad and Alan move towards the hall

Stacey Harrison enters. Stacey, a good-looking, well dressed, highly efficient woman, carries a coat over her arm and a zipped travelling bag.

Alan quickly rushes forward and takes them from her

Stacey Brad! Alan! (*Kissing Brad*) Darling, how are you? Many happy returns! Lovely to see you again!
Brad Did you have a good crossing?
Stacey It was like a mill pond, thank goodness! (*Noticing the presents*) My word, you're a popular man! (*To Alan*) The car's at the door. Bring my things up, there's a darling.
Alan (*hesitating*) Stacey, I'm afraid I've got some bad news for you.
Stacey Peter?

Alan stares at Stacey in amazement

I called in Eaton Place on the way home. That's why I'm late. I should have been here hours ago. (*To Brad*) You've never seen anything like it. The place was ransacked—there's no other word for it!
Brad Alan's been telling me about it.
Alan (*in despair*) Stacey, what on earth are we going to do?
Stacey Well, the first thing we do, darling, is we don't panic and we let Peter think everything's going to be perfectly straight and absolutely lovely, by the time he gets out of hospital.
Alan But that's impossible!
Stacey I know it's impossible, but Peter mustn't think so. I've been on to the workroom and Margo and Lance are meeting me at the house later this evening. I want you to be there too and I've asked Lance to try and get hold of the carpet people . . .
Alan Well—I was just about to run Brad out to Kingsford. He's due there at seven.
Brad Don't worry about me. I can go by train. I'm coming back by train anyway.
Stacey (*to Alan*) No, no, you stick to your arrangements. Take Brad wherever he wants to go and then meet me at Eaton Place. It doesn't matter what time you get there. (*To Brad*) And we'll pick you up later, there's no need to worry about the train.
Brad Are you sure?
Stacey Yes, of course!
Alan I'll get your case, Stacey.
Stacey Here's the key. (*She hands Alan the key*) Most of my things are in

the boot. (*As Alan takes the car key from her she notices the leather strap he is wearing*) Why are you wearing that? Have you hurt your wrist?

Alan (*a shade embarrassed*) Yes, I sprained it. It's nothing.

Stacey What happened?

Alan (*too casually*) Oh—I was helping Peter's housekeeper move a piece of furniture and—rather stupidly I got hold of it the wrong way. (*Looking at the strap*) It's nearly better. I don't know why I'm still wearing this thing.

Alan exits. As he does so he cannot resist giving Brad a casual warning glance

Stacey quietly notices the look and when Alan has departed turns towards Brad

Stacey What's the joke?

Brad Joke? There's no joke.

Stacey Come off it, Brad! What's it all about? What happened to his wrist? How did he do it?

Brad hesitates

Brad Well, if I tell you, will you promise to say nothing about it?

Stacey (*impatiently*) Yes, of course.

Brad Promise?

Stacey Yes, I promise.

Brad A couple of weeks ago a friend of his opened a Ski School in St John's Wood of all places and Alan took it into his head to have some lessons.

Stacey Alan did!

Brad (*amused*) Yes, and during the first lesson he fell off a chair.

Stacey But why on earth does Alan want to take skiing lessons?

Brad He's going to St Moritz for Christmas.

Stacey Alan! He can't afford to go to Pontin's!

Brad He's going with a party. It's a package tour. It's really quite cheap.

Stacey Nonsense, Brad! Don't you believe it! Really, this is very stupid of him! He knows perfectly well we've got masses of work on hand at the moment! What happens if he breaks an arm or a leg?

Brad He'll have to try very hard not to break an arm or a leg. If he doesn't sit on a chair he'll probably be all right.

Stacey smiles and moves to the sofa

Stacey How often does he have these lessons? (*she sits*)

Brad Only twice a week. Now Stacey, don't let on I told you about this! Please! He's a funny sort of chap, and I don't want to fall out with him. (*He joins her on the sofa*)

Stacey (*after a moment, with a friendly little nod*) Yes, all right, darling. I promise.

Brad Now tell me: how did you get on in Paris?

Stacey I enjoyed it, but the weather was disappointing. Incidentally, I've got another birthday present for you. And you'll never guess who from! (*Pause*) Your old friend—or perhaps I should say "young friend"?—Dominic.

Brad (*surprised*) Dominic! Good heavens, fancy Dominic of all people, remembering my birthday! Well—well—wonders will never cease! (*Curiously*) But what happened? Did you look him up while you were in Paris?

Stacey No, of course I didn't, we hardly know each other. Much to my surprise a rather attractive looking girl delivered the parcel just as I was driving away from the hotel.

Brad (*thoughtfully*) Dominic—well, I'm damned! (*Indicating the bottles*) I'll bet a fiver it's another bottle of after-shave!

Stacey You'd lose your bet. It's a picture.

Brad (*a groan*) Not one of Dominic's!

Stacey (*amused*) I'm afraid so.

Brad Oh, my God! Every time he pops over here he brings me one of his monstrosities.

They laugh, then Stacey looks at Brad for a moment, taking hold of his arm

Stacey What did the doctor say?

Brad I told you on the phone. It's nothing serious. He gave me some pills and I've got to have X-rays. He's just an old fuss-pot.

Stacey He's nothing of the sort.

Brad Anyway, the pain's disappeared so there's nothing to worry about. As a matter of fact I've been feeling very frisky.

Stacey (*releasing his arm*) You look fine. Not a day over . . .

Brad Now don't you start! I've had that malarky ever since I woke up this morning. I look sixty, I feel sixty, and worst of all—I am sixty!

Stacey (*noticing the bottles of after-shave*) Well, it certainly looks as if you're going to smell nice in your old age!

Brad Yes, I've got everything from "Eau Savage" to "Hai Karate", to say nothing of Madge's contribution "Butch".

Stacey (*picking up the LP record*) Ravel—*Rhapsodie Espagnole*. Who gave you this?

Brad Alan.

Stacey Doesn't he know by now you're strictly Rodgers and Hammerstein?

Brad Come off it, Stacey!

Stacey laughs and kisses him

Stacey (*putting down the LP*) Now what's all this nonsense about *my* birthday present?

Brad I can't possible accept a whacking great cheque like that!

Stacey Why not, for heaven's sake?

Brad My darling daughter, if I were broke you'd be the first person I'd turn to. But, contrary to general opinion, I'm not broke.

Stacey Well, you should be! I don't know how on earth you manage on that pension. I don't really, Brad!

Brad You know perfectly well how I manage! I play the horses, to say nothing of poker, and I'm dead lucky.

Stacey All right, then play the horses with my birthday present.

Brad I'll do no such thing!

Stacey I'll tell you what you can do! You gamble with the thousand pounds and I'll take half the profit. How's that?

Brad What happens if I lose?

Stacey You won't—you never do! (*Smiling at him and affectionately touching his cheek*) Now tell me what that nice mother-in-law of mine wanted. I just caught sight of her getting into a cab.

Brad (*indicating the after-shave lotion*) She brought me a present.

Stacey That was thoughtful of her.

Brad Yes, it was, but—I really think it was just an excuse to tell me about the divorce.

Stacey looks at him

She saw your letter on Philip's desk and put two and two together.

Stacey (*laughing*) Yes, she would! Dear Madge! I know exactly how she feels. (*Rising*) But I hope she doesn't think that a concerted effort on everyone's part will make me change my mind. (*She goes to the writing table and picks up several letters*)

Brad I doubt very much whether she's labouring under that delusion. (*Pause*) Stacey, it's none of my business but—why have you suddenly decided on a divorce?

Stacey (*not unpleasantly*) I haven't suddenly decided, I've been thinking about it for some time. And you're quite right, darling. It's none of your business.

Brad Is there someone else?

Stacey (*looking at one of the letters she has opened*) No, there isn't.

Brad Would you tell me if there was?

Stacey No, Brad, I wouldn't.

Alan enters carrying a suitcase, several pairs of shoes, a cardigan, and a white linen "sack" which obviously contains a picture. The sack is tied with picture cord

Brad leans the "sack" against one of the chairs

Alan I'll take these things into the bedroom.

Stacey Would you, darling . . . (*She puts the letters back on the writing table*)

Alan exits

Brad goes to the chair and attempts to open the sack. He has difficulty with the cord

Has Alan been looking after you while I've been away?

Brad I haven't seen a great deal of him, he's been out most of the time.

(*Still attempting to untie the sack*) He's a funny sort of chap, isn't he?

Stacey goes to the trolley and picks up a knife

Stacey Yes, you said that before. What do you mean, funny?

Brad Oh, I don't know. I was just talking to Madge about him. He's got very good taste and he's clever, but—there are times when he strikes me as being—well, something of an opportunist.

Stacey (*thoughtfully*) Yes, I know what you mean. Try this, darling.

Brad (*taking the knife from her and cutting the cord*) And my God, when he loses his temper! All hell's let loose!

Stacey (*laughing*) Yes, I know. I've experienced it. But to be fair, Alan's had a pretty rough ride in recent years. His gallery folded—which was a bitter disappointment to him—and he lost a great deal of money very quickly. Mostly other people's. That sort of thing has an effect on you.

Brad Yes, I'm sure it does. (*Dismissing the matter and finally untying the sack*) Anyway, he's a damn good cook, I'll say that for him.

The picture is now revealed. It is a medium size oil painting, badly painted but imposingly framed. It depicts a small group of children staring up at the Eiffel Tower

My God, what's Dominic playing at? It's even worse than last year's efforts. (*He hands Stacey the knife*)

Stacey Wasn't that the Eiffel Tower too?

Brad (*placing the picture on the sofa*) It's always the Eiffel Tower!

Stacey No, the time before last, if you remember, we had the nude reading *Paris Match*.

Brad (*exasperated*) Yes, but even she was leaning against the Eiffel Tower.

Stacey (*laughing*) If I remember rightly it was the Tower that was leaning!

Stacey puts the knife down on the side table

Alan enters. He stops dead on seeing the picture

What do you think of this masterpiece, Alan?

Alan picks up the picture and stares at it

Alan Is it a birthday present?

Brad Yes. From an ex-pupil of mine.

Alan Was he expelled? Which Tower is it? Pisa—the Eiffel—or the Post Office? (*Peering at the signature*) Whichever it is Dominic—is that his name?—ought to jump off it. (*He returns the picture to the sofa*)

Brad You'll hardly believe it, Alan, but when Dominic lived in Kingsford he did some terribly clever work; really original. Then one day he packed his job in, left his wife and kids, and went to live in Paris. He's been turning out rubbish like this ever since. (*Shaking his head*) I shall just have to flog it, I'm afraid.

Alan If you can flog this, dear boy, you can flog anything—and the sooner we go into business together the better. (*Glances at his watch*) Brad, I think we ought to be making a move.

Brad Yes, of course.
Alan (*to Stacey*) See you at Peter's. I'll get there as soon as I can.
Stacey There's no hurry, I shall be ages anyway. (*To Brad*) Enjoy yourself
and don't drink too much.
Brad Make your mind up.
Stacey (*laughing*) We'll pick you up later.

Brad and Alan exit

*Stacey now takes a critical look at the room, wondering if anything has been
changed during her absence. She switches on a table lamp, turns off the main
light, tidies the cushions, straightens one of the pictures, moves a chair into a
different position, examines Brad's birthday cards and presents, and then
takes several of the cards and the spray bottle of after-shave lotion across to a
side table. She puts the cards and the after-shave lotion on the table, switches
on another lamp, and then draws the full-length curtains across the window.
Having done this she turns and surveys the dimly lit room once again, her eye
finally coming to rest on the painting. She returns, and picking up the picture
goes into the bedroom with it*

Stacey exits

*Pause. The bedroom door is heard to close, then noises from the bathroom.
The telephone rings, and continues to ring for a few moments. After a long
pause the front door buzzer is heard. The telephone bell continues, and also
the front door buzzer*

Stacey enters, wearing a bath-robe and turban

*She hesitates, looking first towards the hall, then at the telephone. Finally she
moves to the latter, but it stops ringing just as she reaches it. She turns
towards the hall. As she reaches the alcove she pauses, suddenly conscious of
what she is wearing. She is undecided whether to answer the door or not. The
buzzer is heard again. She quickly takes off the turban, shakes her hair into
position*

Stacey exits into the hall and opens the front door

(*off*) Why, hello, Philip! I'll be with you in a minute—I've got the bath
running.

*Stacey comes back into the room and quickly disappears into the bedroom.
Philip Harrison enters, slowly looking about him. It is the first time he
has been in the apartment. He is dependable, faintly sardonic at times, in
his late thirties*

Pause. Philip continues to take stock of his surroundings

Stacey enters, wearing an attractive housecoat

Stacey I'm so sorry . . .
Philip I bumped into Brad. He said you were back.
Stacey Yes. I've just arrived.

Slight pause

Philip You look very well, Stacey. Did you have a good trip?
Stacey Very—but the weather wasn't so good.
Philip In Rome?
Stacey I didn't get as far as Rome. Except for a week-end in Cannes I stayed in Paris most of the time.
Philip You appear to have taken quite a liking to Paris. What's this—your fourth trip this year?
Stacey My fifth.
Philip You used to say it was terribly noisy and exorbitantly expensive.
Stacey It still is.

Tiny pause

Philip Where did you stay, at the Lancaster?
Stacey No. The George Cinq.
Philip (*surprised*) The George Cinq? That doesn't sound like you.

Another pause. They take each other in

Stacey You got my letter?
Philip Yes, I did. That's why I'm here.
Stacey I didn't know whether to write to you or not.
Philip Why did you?
Stacey (*faintly surprised by the question*) I wanted you to know that I've made my mind up and I thought perhaps it was kinder to write rather than wait until I got back.
Philip Oh, I see. From your letter I thought perhaps there might be a degree of urgency.
Stacey No, there's no urgency. (*Tiny pause*) But I shan't change my mind.
Philip Such a remote possibility never occurred to me. But I must admit I'm surprised. I thought you were reasonably happy with the present arrangement?
Stacey Whatever gave you that impression? I told you, before I went away, that I was thinking about a divorce.
Philip Yes, I know you did.
Stacey But you didn't believe me?
Philip Yes, I believed you. But I thought, I hoped, you'd decide against it.
Stacey Well, I'm sorry, Philip, but I haven't. (*Tiny pause*) Please sit down.

Pause. Philip sits on the sofa

Philip Is there someone else?
Stacey That's the second time today I've been asked that question.
Philip Is there someone else?

After a moment, Stacey turns away from him, moves to a chair and sits

Stacey No, there isn't.

Another pause

Philip Did you see Gerald Waddington while you were in Paris?
Stacey Yes. He flew over last Friday.
Philip (*surprised*) But I thought he lived there?
Stacey No, he's living over here at the moment.
Philip I didn't realize that.
Stacey He's sold his place in Paris and bought a farm in the Cotswolds, near Chipping Norton.
Philip Good God! Gerald Waddington in the Cotswolds!
Stacey He commutes, from Curzon Street.
Philip That's more like it.
Stacey He rang me up from the airport on Friday morning and said, "I'm in Paris for the day, Stace. We're having lunch together. I'll pick you up at one o'clock." Before I could tell him I already had a date he rang off.
Philip He would (*After a moment*) He still calls you Stace?
Stacey I'm afraid so. I've tried to break him of the habit but I haven't been very successful.
Philip Perhaps you should try ringing off for a change. (*Tiny pause*) Did he ask you to marry him?
Stacey (*after a momentary hesitation*) No, but he's going to.
Philip And what happens then?
Stacey I don't want to marry anyone, not at the moment.
Philip Then why do you want a divorce?
Stacey (*hesitantly*) I just don't want to go on like this.
Philip Why not?
Stacey (*rising*) Philip, you know me. I have a tidy mind. I like everything to be . . .
Philip (*interrupting her*) But I don't know you, Stacey. Surely that's our problem? (*He rises*)
Stacey (*irritated, sensing the possible start of a scene*) Don't let's start bickering, Philip! Not now, please!
Philip I haven't the slightest wish to start bickering. I'm not very good at it anyway. (*A pause, then quietly*) I take it—this time—you really have made your mind up?
Stacey Yes . . .
Philip Quite definitely?
Stacey (*firmly*) Quite definitely.

They stand looking at each other

Philip Well, in that case, there's nothing more to be said. If that's what you want, Stacey . . .
Stacey That's what I want.
Philip All right. Then that's it. (*He consults his watch*) I'm meeting a client at seven-thirty and I'm sure you've a hundred and one things to see to. (*He goes towards the hall*) Please let me know if I can help you in any way.

Stacey Thank you, Philip.

Philip stares at her for a brief moment then exits

Stacey stands looking towards the hall. It is obvious that she is still puzzled by Philip's attitude. There is even a tiny suggestion of suspicion on her face as she turns and, still deep in thought, goes to the bedroom

Stacey exits

A very long pause

Charles Venner slowly enters from the dining room. He stands framed in the doorway, quietly taking note of the contents of the room. Venner is a smartly dressed man in the early forties

When he finally moves into the room it becomes obvious that he is a stranger to his surroundings. He glances towards the bedroom then crosses to the table near the sofa. He picks up an antique silver box and is casually examining it when the front door buzzer is heard. Venner freezes. He looks towards the hall. Pause. Door buzzer. Suddenly Venner hears another noise—this time from the bedroom—and for a split second he is undecided what to do. Then he hears the same noise again and putting down the cigarette box quickly turns and disappears behind the curtains

Stacey enters from the bedroom and goes to the hall, to open the front door

Telegraph Boy (*off*) Telegram.
Stacey (*off*) Oh—thank you.

Stacey returns, holding a telegram, and moves into the room. Almost simultaneously she becomes aware of a slight movement, quickly turns and looks towards the kitchen

Slight pause. It is obvious that Stacey is now a shade suspicious; just vaguely conscious of the fact that there might possibly be someone else in the flat. She thrusts the telegram into her pocket and moves towards the kitchen. As she passes the writing table and draws level with the kitchen Venner suddenly springs from behind the curtains and grabs hold of her. Taken by surprise, Stacey makes a desperate attempt to free herself. As she struggles her right hand gropes wildly across the surface of the table. She finds the bottle of after-shave lotion and brings it close to Venner's chin, squirting the contents of the bottle directly into his eyes. With a curse Venner releases her, his hands flying instinctively to his face. After a slightly confused hesitation Stacey rushes away from him. Venner quickly recovers and by the time Stacey has reached the table he has caught up with her again. As he closes in on her Stacey suddenly sees the knife on the table and quickly picks it up. Venner's eyes are still blurred and he fails to see what she is holding

Stacey Keep away! Keep away from me!

His hands have reached her throat and he is about to throttle her when she plunges the knife into his body. Venner releases his grip, staggers, then with a groan collapses. Stacey stands staring down at Venner's body. It is the first time she has really seen her assailant and she is visibly shaken

Oh, my God . . .

Pause. She slowly turns and, with her eyes still on the body, picks up the phone. She hesitates, then with a trembling hand starts to dial for the police. When the number is ringing out she suddenly panics and quickly rings off. Stacey is still shaking, holding on to the table for support, when the door buzzer is heard. Stacey looks across at the hall. Door buzzer is heard again. She moves down towards the alcove, not sure whether to answer the door or not. Suddenly she hears Philip calling to her from outside the front door

Philip (*off*) It's Philip, Stacey!

Immediately Stacey recognizes Philip's voice she runs out into the hall and opens the front door

Stacey (*off*) Philip, for God's sake, come quickly!

Philip enters, followed by Stacey. He takes one look at Venner then turns to Stacey

Philip What happened?

Stacey I was in the bedroom . . . He must have had a key to the back door, unless it was unlocked. (*Staring at the body*) He tried to strangle me . . .

Philip (*concerned*) Are you all right?

Stacey Yes. Yes, but it was such a terrible shock. One minute we were struggling and then . . . (*She stops; staring at Venner*) Is he dead?

Philip looks at her for a moment, then he crosses down to Venner and examines him. There is a long pause

Philip (*looking at her again*) Who is he, Stacey?

Stacey I—don't know. I've never seen him before. Is he dead?

Philip continues looking at her, then he slowly nods his head as—

the Lights fade to a Black-out

SCENE 2

The same. About ten-thirty the next morning

Venner's body has now been removed. There is a tray with coffee, etc, on a side table and copies of the morning newspapers are strewn across the sofa. Brad enters with Philip, having just let him in

Brad . . . I took her a cup of tea but she didn't even know I was in the room.

Philip What time was that?

Brad About nine o'clock. I haven't heard a sound so I imagine she's still asleep.

Philip I think perhaps you'd better wake her, Brad. The Inspector's due at ten-thirty.

Brad Yes, all right. (*Returning to the table*) I've just been having some coffee. Would you like a cup?

Philip No, thank you.

Brad Philip, what happened last night, when the police arrived? Were they difficult?

Philip No, on the contrary. They were helpful and very considerate. Fortunately I'd met the Inspector before which was quite a help.

Brad goes to the sofa and gathers up the newspapers

But I'm afraid she's going to get rather a lot of publicity in the next week or so.

Brad (*indicating the newspapers*) Well, she hasn't done too badly this morning, by the look of things!

The telephone rings

Oh Lord, here we go again! This damn thing's never stopped ringing. (*Going to the phone*) Oh, I forgot—your mother rang up . . .

Philip You do surprise me.

Brad She was on the phone for fifteen minutes.

Philip Only fifteen minutes? She must have laryngitis.

Brad (*lifting the receiver*) five-eight-nine seven-eight-four-three . . . Oh, hello, Gerald! . . . Yes, I expect you have! (*He turns and looks at Philip*) She's perfectly all right, old boy, there's nothing to worry about . . . No, no, truly . . . I'd tell you . . . Yes, of course I will . . . She's perfectly all right, I assure you . . . Well, she's resting at the moment and I'd rather not disturb her . . . It was—it was indeed . . . What's that? . . . We haven't the faintest idea who he is, Gerald— no-one seems to know anything about him . . . (*Pause*) That's very kind of you, I'm sure she'll appreciate it . . . Yes, of course I will, but I expect she'll talk to you herself later in the day . . . Thank you for ringing. (*He replaces the receiver*)

Philip Gerald Waddington?

Brad Yes. He wanted to know how *Stace* was.

Slight pause

Philip Does Stacey see much of him these days?

Brad I don't think so. Certainly not as much as she used to.

Philip I'm told he's living over here at the moment.

Brad Yes, he's got a place in Curzon Street and he's bought a farm in the Cotswolds. Near Broadway or Chipping something or other. He's always trying something new. Do you remember that antique shop of his in Cambridge?

Philip It was a failure.

Brad The shop was, but the lease wasn't. He made a packet out of it. The year before that it was a pet shop in Harrogate, next door to Woolworth's. That was another catastrophe, or it would have been if Woolworth's hadn't wanted to extend. Then he opened that ghastly restaurant.

Philip I don't remember the restaurant.

Brad You're lucky. I only had one meal there but I've never forgotten it. I was on the loo for six hours. Cross my heart, old boy! Stacey rang him up the next day and said, "For God's sake keep the recipe, Gerald, in case there's an autopsy".

Philip Where was it?

Brad The restaurant? In Pimlico. Chez Gerald—French food to take away. I think he was frightened the customers might die on the premises. You can't beat our Gerald! He's literally the only man I know who's made a fortune by never putting a foot right.

Another pause

Philip I suppose you know why I called here last night? Stacey wrote me a letter saying she wanted a divorce.

Brad nods

When I received the letter I jumped to the conclusion—the wrong conclusion, apparently—that she wanted to marry Gerald.

Brad I don't think she wants to marry anyone at the moment.

Philip Then why does she want the divorce?

Brad I don't know. You'd better ask her. (*Deliberately changing the subject*) Philip, I'd like to pay Peter Lockwood a visit some time this morning and since I'd rather not leave Stacey on her own, I was wondering if you . . .

Stacey enters from the bedroom

Stacey Why don't you want to leave me on my own, Brad?

Stacey is wearing yet another attractive housecoat. Although she has taken trouble with her hair and make-up she still looks tense and drawn

Philip Hello, Stacey!

Brad (*anxiously*) How are you, my dear? How do you feel?

Stacey (*almost a shade defiantly*) I feel fine.

Brad Come and sit down. (*Moving to an armchair*) Let me make you a cup of tea.

Stacey Now stop fussing, Brad! Please! I'm perfectly all right!

Stacey moves to the sofa. Brad looks across at Philip, not quite sure what to say next

Brad Are you sure I can't get you anything?

Stacey No. No, really, darling. I'll have some coffee later. Who was that on the phone?

Brad Alan, Madge, Gerald Waddington, and about every newspaper in Fleet Street. Take your pick.

Stacey What did Alan want?

Brad He's having trouble with the carpet people, he wants to talk to you.

Stacey I'll phone him later. Did he say how Peter was?

Brad I gather he's a lot better. The old boy telephoned his housekeeper this morning so there must be quite a big improvement. I thought I'd slip round to the Clinic and see if there's anything I can do for him.

Stacey That's a good idea, Brad. And tell him not to worry about the house. Everything's under control.

Brad I'll be back in about an hour.

Stacey If I'm not here I'll be at Peter's. And don't worry about me, I feel fine now, truly, darling.

Brad exits

Tiny pause

Philip How do you really feel?

Stacey (*hesitantly*) I don't honestly know. I lay in bed last night thinking about what happened—I couldn't believe it. I just couldn't believe that I'd—actually killed someone.

Philip gives a sympathetic little nod

Philip Aren't you going to have any breakfast?

Stacey I don't really feel like any.

Philip I should try and eat something.

Stacey (*after a moment, hesitatingly*) I want to thank you, Philip.

Philip What for?

Stacey For last night. For taking charge of everything—for talking to the police the way you did. I don't know what on earth I would have done if you hadn't turned up.

Philip You'd have eventually pulled yourself together. There was nothing else you could do.

Stacey I'm not so sure. For a moment, just a brief moment, I almost lost complete control of myself. It was only when I heard your voice that . . . Well, I want you to know that I'm grateful.

Philip I'm just glad that I came back when I did.

Stacey Incidentally, why did you? I suddenly thought of that this morning. Why did you come back?

Philip There was something I wanted to say to you, about the house. But it's not important.

The door buzzer sounds. Stacey turns towards the hall

That'll be the Inspector. Shall I let him in?

Stacey nods

Philip exits

Stacey takes a cigarette from the box on the table. She looks at the cigarette for a moment, her thoughts obviously elsewhere, then, suddenly hearing voices, she replaces the cigarette in the box and turns towards the hall

Philip (*off*) Good morning, Inspector.
Lennox (*off*) Good morning, sir.

Philip enters with Detective-Inspector Lennox. Lennox is in his late thirties; a well-spoken, shrewd-looking man. He carries a briefcase

Good morning, Mrs Harrison.
Stacey Good morning, Inspector.
Lennox (*looking at Stacey*) If I may say so, Madam, you appear to have survived your unfortunate experience remarkably well.
Stacey Don't let my make-up deceive you, Inspector, I'm still very shaky.
Lennox Yes, indeed, I expect you are. (*He looks at his case, undecided whether to put it down or not*)
Stacey Please sit down.
Lennox Thank you.

Lennox takes stock of the room, finally deciding to sit on the sofa

Philip Well—were you finally able to identify our visitor?
Lennox (*putting case on the sofa*) Identify him, sir?
Philip Yes. Last night, if I remember rightly, there was some doubt about his identity.
Lennox Was there? I didn't realize that.
Philip After you left I asked the Sergeant who he was and he said . . . (*A sudden thought*) Perhaps he was just being evasive.

Lennox dismisses the Sergeant's evasiveness with a smile

Lennox Yes, well—we identified him all right. His name's Venner.
Philip Venner?
Lennox Yes. Charles Venner. Have you heard the name before, sir?
Philip No, I haven't.
Lennox Madam?

Lennox looks at Stacey who quietly shakes her head

Lennox He was staying at a hotel in Bloomsbury, the Winston.
Philip In Bedford Square?
Lennox That's right. Apparently he checked in the hotel—but I'll tell you about Mr Venner later. (*Pause*) Mrs Harrison, I understand that you left Paris by car yesterday morning and arrived home soon after six?
Stacey That's right.
Lennox Was your husband here when you arrived?
Stacey (*with a glance at Philip*) No.
Philip I don't live here, Inspector. My wife and I are separated.

Lennox Oh. Oh, I see.

Stacey My father was here and the young man you met last night—Alan Kyle. They've been staying here while I've been away.

Lennox And there was no-one else in the apartment?

Stacey No.

Lennox Haven't you any help?

Stacey Yes, I have an *au pair*, but she's away at the moment.

Lennox I see. Now tell me what happened after your father and Mr Kyle left for Kingsford.

Stacey My father used to be head of the Kingsford Art Centre. It was his birthday yesterday, and some of the students gave a party for him.

Lennox Go on, Mrs Harrison.

Stacey Well—shortly after my father left, Philip—my husband—arrived.

Lennox That would be about a quarter to seven?

Stacey Yes. About a quarter to seven.

Lennox Were you expecting your husband?

Stacey (*after a momentary hesitation*) No.

Lennox Were you expecting any visitors?

Stacey No, I wasn't.

Lennox (*to Philip*) How long did you stay here?

Philip Oh—not very long. About ten minutes, I should imagine.

Stacey After my husband left I went back into the bedroom. A few minutes later a boy arrived with a telegram. I was just about to open the telegram when I heard a noise in the kitchen. At least, I thought it was in the kitchen. (*Her voice becoming tense as she recalls the incident*) I crossed over to the kitchen and—Venner, did you say his name was?—immediately sprang from behind the curtains and tried to strangle me. Fortunately there was a knife on that table and—I—was able to . . .

Philip My wife picked up the knife and defended herself with it. I'm quite sure, under similar circumstances your wife would have done precisely the same.

Lennox I'm a bachelor, sir. (*Slowly rising*) Mrs Harrison, would you mind showing me exactly where you were standing when Venner materialized so suddenly?

Philip glances at Lennox, a shade surprised both by the use of the word "materialized" and the Inspector's inflection. Stacey hesitates, then she goes over to the table and stands facing the dining room door. Her back is partly turned towards the curtains. Lennox joins her. He looks at the curtains, moving them slightly with his hand

Stacey About here . . .

Slight pause

Lennox So when Venner grabbed hold of you, you didn't actually see him?

Stacey No, I didn't. There were very few lights on at the time and he took me completely by surprise.

Lennox It was only later, when he was dead, that you were able to get a good look at him?

Stacey (*puzzled*) Well—yes.
Lennox And you'd never seen him before?
Stacey No, never.

Pause. Lennox is looking at Stacey

Lennox You're quite sure about that?
Stacey (*puzzled*) That I'd never seen him before? Yes, I'm quite sure.

Lennox continues looking at Stacey, then finally with a quite, "Thank you, madam," he returns to the sofa and picks up his briefcase. Philip watches him, obviously puzzled
        (*Hesitantly*) Don't you believe me, Inspector?

Lennox (*not looking at her*) I'd like to believe you, Mrs Harrison—
Stacey That's not what I asked you!
Lennox —but I'm finding it a little difficult under the circumstances.
Philip (*moving down to Lennox; faintly aggressive*) What circumstances?

The Inspector turns

Lennox Charles Venner arrived from Paris yesterday afternoon.
Philip From Paris?
Lennox Yes, sir. He was on the Air France Flight that landed at Heathrow at three twenty-three. He picked up a Hertz car with a driver and checked in the Winston Hotel at approximately five o'clock. The first thing he did was order a dry martini and make a phone call. (*Indicating the phone*) To this number.

Philip looks at Stacey

Stacey This number?
Lennox Yes. Five-eight-nine Seven-eight-four-three. That is your number, Mrs Harrison?
Stacey Yes, but—why should he ring my number?
Lennox Presumably he wanted to talk to you.
Stacey But I've already told you I've never . . . Who did he talk to?
Lennox No-one. There was no reply.
Stacey (*suddenly*) The phone did ring! I've just remembered. It rang and I didn't answer it! I didn't get to it in time.
Lennox When was this?
Stacey Just as my husband arrived. About a quarter to seven.
Lennox (*shaking his head*) The call I'm talking about was made within five or six minutes of Venner arriving at the hotel. Five o'clock, ten past five at the latest. (*Opening his briefcase*) However, the phone call's not all that important. What is important, is that (*taking a diary out of his case*) this morning we found this diary in a sports jacket belonging to the dead man. (*Opening the diary*) I'd like to read you what he wrote in the diary on Sunday, November the eighteenth—that's a week last Sunday. (*Reading from the diary*) "Had lunch with Stacey. Yet another row. We can't go on like this. Wish I knew what the devil was the matter with her . . ."

Stacey moves down to Lennox. It is difficult to tell by her expression whether she is dumbfounded or merely embarrassed

Here's another reference to you, Mrs Harrison. (*Turning the pages of the diary*) Written the day before yesterday. (*Looking at her*) The day before yesterday, Mrs Harrison. (*Reading*) "Hope to see Stacey tomorrow. Will try and make her see reason this time. Must confess I'm not optimistic . . ." (*He looks at Stacey again, then slowly closing the diary puts it back in his briefcase*)

Stacey (*tensely, shaking her head*) I—I don't understand this. He must be referring to someone else . . .

Lennox (*sceptically*) Someone else called Stacey? (*Quietly*) Mrs Harrison, sometimes in a situation of this kind people overlook things, or say things which at a later date they have cause to regret. (*To Philip*) I'm sure you know that only too well, sir.

Stacey What are you suggesting?

Lennox I'm not suggesting anything, madam. But if by any chance you have inadvertently . . .

Stacey (*interrupting him, intensely angry*) I think you are! You're suggesting that I knew this man, that I knew he was coming here, that we had a row, and that I deliberately killed him!

Lennox (*somewhat taken aback by her attack*) I did not suggest that, Mrs Harrison. But is that what happened?

Stacey I've told you what happened! I'd never seen this man before! I'd never even heard the name Charles Venner until you mentioned it this morning.

Pause

Lennox I see. Thank you. (*Closing the interview, fastening his briefcase*) The chances are I shall want to see you again, Mrs Harrison, later in the day. Will you be here?

Stacey Yes, I will.

Lennox nods and exits. Philip hesitates, then follows him into the hall

Stacey looks tense and distinctly worried as she slowly moves to the sofa, where she stands deep in thought

Philip returns

Pause. Philip looks at her earnestly, and after a moment she raises her eyes and gives him a long look, as—

The Lights slowly fade to a Black-out

SCENE 3

The same. Twenty-four hours later; Friday morning

Alan is sitting at the writing table sorting through a collection of fabrics. The table is a mass of account books, documents, samples of curtain materials, etc.

It is obvious that Alan is agitated and his thoughts elsewhere. From time to time he runs his fingers through his hair, looks at his watch, and glances towards the bedrooms. Suddenly the door buzzer is heard and, with a welcome sigh of relief at the interruption, he gets up and goes out into the hall. We hear Madge's voice immediately the front door is opened.

Madge (*off*) Good morning, Alan. Is Stacey in?
Alan (*off*) No, Madge, I'm afraid she isn't.
Madge (*off*) Well, where is she?

Madge enters, followed by Alan

Alan I'm afraid we don't know where she is.
Madge (*querulously*) What do you mean, you don't know?
Alan We just don't know. She's disappeared.
Madge Disappeared!
Alan Yes—no-one's seen her. Not since yesterday morning. We're all very, very worried.
Madge But what on earth's happened? Why has Stacey suddenly taken it into her head to disappear?
Alan Don't you know what's happened?

Madge shakes her head

Stacey knew Venner.
Madge Venner?
Alan The man who broke into the flat. She was a friend of his. That's why he came here.
Madge (*shocked*) I don't believe that!
Alan I'm afraid it's true. The police found a diary of Venner's. It had several references to Stacey in it. (*Moving to the writing table*) That's why Brad's in such a state. Why we're all so worried. The worst possible thing she could have done was to have run away like this!
Madge (*springing to Stacey's defence*) When did she "run away", as you put it?
Alan Yesterday morning, after the police questioned her. She was obviously scared to death and decided to . . .
Madge Wait a minute! Were you here when she was questioned?
Alan No, I was at the workshop.
Madge Then how do you know she was scared?
Alan Because immediately after the Inspector left she got rid of Philip, packed a bag, took her car out of the garage and disappeared. Now I ask you! Why on earth would she do that if she wasn't scared?
Madge (*shaking her head*) I don't know! But I do know this doesn't sound like Stacey. If she's got a problem she faces up to it.
Alan Yes, but this isn't just a case of "Shall we have chintz, darling, or velvet?" If she isn't already facing a murder charge, the chances are she will be by this time tomorrow.
Madge Did she admit that she knew this man?

Alan No, she didn't. But the Inspector said . . .
Madge I'm not interested in what the Inspector said! What did Stacey say?
Alan She said she'd never seen Venner before. She'd never heard of him.
Madge Well, that's good enough for me!

Brad enters. He is dressed for going out and looks both worried and agitated

Brad Oh, hello, Madge! I wondered who it was . . .
Madge Brad, you don't believe this story about Stacey? That she's deliberately disappeared?

Brad hesitates, then gives a little shrug

Brad I don't know.
Madge Do you think she knew this man Venner?
Brad I just don't know what to believe!
Madge Yes, well—if Stacey says she's never seen this man before then she's never seen him before! So far as I'm concerned, it's as simple as that!
Brad Unfortunately it's not as simple as that so far as the police are concerned. (*He sighs*) Madge, where are you going from here?
Madge Wimpole Street.
Brad Oh, good. I've got to be at the hospital at eleven. Could you drop me?
Madge Yes, of course.
Brad (*to Alan*) I don't know what time I'll be back. I'll try and phone you, in case you've heard anything.
Alan If I'm not here I shall be at Peter's
Madge (*to Alan*) Immediately Stacey turns up—and she will!—give me a ring.
Alan Yes, all right, Madge. I'll do that.
Madge Now don't you forget! Right now she's going to need every friend she's got. And that includes you, young man!
Alan Yes, Madge! I promise!

Madge exits with Brad

Alan returns to the table and picks up a sample of curtain material. He looks at the sample for a moment, his thoughts obviously elsewhere, then he puts it down and sits at the table. He opens one of the account books, stares at it, then rises and crosses over to the drinks trolley. He picks up a bottle of Scotch, hesitates, glances at his watch, looks at the bottle again, then with a shrug and a "What the hell!" he mixes himself a whisky and soda. He is about to drink when he suddenly hears the opening and closing of the front door. He puts down his glass and turns towards the hall

Stacey enters carrying a small overnight case as well as a coat and handbag. She appears tense and extremely tired as, almost ignoring Alan, she moves to the sofa

Alan Stacey! (*Moving towards her*) Where have you been?

Stacey does not answer; instead she puts down the case and handbag and throws her coat over the arm of the sofa

We've all been out of our minds with worry! Poor Brad's been in a hell of a state!

Stacey (*softly*) Yes, I know. I've seen him—and Madge. I've just been talking to them.

Alan The police have never been off the doorstep! They called here twice last night and this morning . . .

Stacey Alan, I'm very tired! Now, please—be a darling. (*Offering him a car key*) Don't ask questions. Just put the car away for me.

Alan Stacey, I don't think you realize what's been happening during the past twenty-four hours!

Stacey Darling, please! Do as I ask! (*Pause*) I'll see you later at Eaton Place.

Alan hesitates, obviously puzzled and somewhat alarmed by Stacey's mood

Alan (*reluctantly, taking the key*) Yes, all right.

Stacey picks up her case and goes into the bedroom. Alan stands for a little while, his eyes on the bedroom, then with a glance at the car key he is holding he turns and goes into the hall

Pause

Stacey comes out of the bedroom and crossing down to the sofa picks up her coat. She looks worried and distinctly agitated as she searches the pockets of her coat. It is quite obvious that she is looking for something she has recently mislaid. To her dismay the pockets are empty and after looking behind the loose cushions she commences to run her hand down the side of the sofa

Suddenly voices are heard and Stacey, taken by surprise turns and looks towards the hall. As Alan appears with the visitor, she quickly straightens herself and moves away from the sofa

Alan enters with Gerald Waddington

Stacey, it's Gerald Waddington . . .

Gerald Waddington is in the early forties. A smart, amiable looking man who, over the years, has tried—not very successfully—to conceal his faint North Country accent

Gerald Hello, Stace! Hope I haven't dropped in at an awkward moment?

Stacey No, of course not! Lovely to see you, Gerald! Come along in! Thank you, Alan.

Alan goes

Gerald (*moving down to Stacey; concerned*) Stace, how are you? (*Kissing her*) How are you, my dear? Let me take a good look at you . . . My God, what an experience! What a terrible thing to have happened! But I must say, you've survived it better than I expected. A devil of a lot better!

Stacey I knew you'd say that!

Gerald No, really—I mean it. Honestly. You look super.

Stacey Well, I don't feel super! But I'm alive!

Gerald I tried to see you yesterday. I called round twice, but there was no reply.

Stacey Yes, I'm sorry, Gerald. I was out.

Gerald Have the newspapers been hounding you?

Stacey No, I must say, on the whole, they've been pretty good.

Slight pause. Gerald is about to say something, then obviously changes his mind

Gerald How's Brad? I caught a glimpse of him at the beginning of the week. I didn't think he looked quite his usual self.

Stacey He hasn't been a hundred per cent.

Stacey now realizes that Gerald has something on his mind and is hesitating before coming to the point

What is it, Gerald?

Gerald (*hesitantly*) Stace, that man—the chap that broke into your flat . . .

Stacey Venner . . .

Gerald Yes. There's a picture of him in one of this morning's newspapers.

Stacey Yes, I know. I've seen it.

Gerald Well—perhaps I've got hold of the wrong end of the stick, but when I spoke to Brad about what happened he gave me to understand that you'd never seen Venner before. That he was a stranger to you.

Stacey That's right. He was.

Gerald (*puzzled*) You mean—the first time you saw him was when he tried to kill you?

Stacey Yes.

Gerald You'd never actually set eyes on him before then?

Stacey No, never.

Pause

Gerald (*a shade embarrassed*) Stace, I'm awfully sorry, but I'm afraid that's not true.

Stacey Not true? What do you mean?

Gerald That day—the day we had lunch together in Paris . . .

Stacey Yes?

Gerald I picked you up at your hotel, the George Cinq, remember?

Stacey That's right.

Gerald I was standing near the cocktail bar, waiting for you. You came down in the elevator.

Stacey Yes, I remember . . .

Gerald Well, surely—Venner was with you.
Stacey (*apparently amazed*) Venner? With me?
Gerald Yes. What I mean is—he was in the lift with you.
Stacey Venner was?
Gerald Yes.

Slight pause

Stacey I don't remember that.
Gerald He walked past me. I thought he was a friend of yours so I had a good look at him. (*Watching her*) It was Venner. Definitely. I recognized his picture, as soon as I saw it.

Pause

Stacey Are you sure you didn't see him somewhere else?
Gerald No, it was in Paris. At your hotel.

Another pause

Stacey Have you mentioned this to anyone?
Gerald No, of course not.

They are still facing each other, Gerald staring at her with obvious interest

Stacey (*quietly*) I think you must be mistaken, Gerald.

She turns away from him and after a moment Gerald gives a resigned little shrug

Gerald All right, Stace. For you—I'm mistaken. (*Dismissing the subject*) Now how about having dinner with me one day this week?
Stacey This week's awfully difficult. With being away I'm absolutely up to my eyes in work.
Gerald Come along! It'll do you good. Take your mind off things. How about Sunday night? We could drive out into the country some place.
Stacey Yes, all right. Sunday. Pick me up about seven.
Gerald (*delighted*) Super.

As they cross the room together, the door buzzer is heard

Stacey Excuse me.

Stacey exits to the hall, re-entering after a moment with Philip

Gerald (*in a friendly tone*) Hello, Phil. Nice to see you. How are you keeping these days?
Philip I'm well, thank you. And you?
Gerald I'm fine. And congratulations.
Philip (*curtly*) On what?
Gerald That Liverpool case. I didn't think you were going to get away with it.

Philip gives him a look

Philip I don't think anyone "got away with it". But I'm glad we surprised you. (*He moves to the sofa*)

Gerald smiles at Stacey, not at all put out by the rebuff

Gerald See you Sunday, Stace.
Stacey Yes, darling. (*Affectionately, taking hold of his arm*) I'll look forward to it. Any time after seven.
Gerald Seven on the dot! Nice to see you again, Phil.

Gerald and Stacey exit

Philip turns and looks towards the hall, waiting for Stacey to return

After a moment Stacey enters

They take each other in

Philip What happened to you yesterday?
Stacey (*resenting his tone*) What do you mean—what happened to me?
Philip (*angrily*) You know perfectly well what I mean! Where the hell did you go?
Stacey I—I went down to Brighton. I stayed the night there.
Philip Don't you realize the police have been looking all over the place for you! (*Moving to her*) Why on earth did you do a stupid thing like that?
Stacey I wanted to get away! I was frightened and tired and I just didn't want to answer any more questions!
Philip But don't you realize that by running away like that . . .
Stacey I didn't run away!
Philip Of course you ran away! You panicked! And it was bloody stupid of you! (*Pause*) I saw the Inspector last night. Twice. The second time he was with Chief Superintendent Horton.

Stacey looks at him

Horton's in charge of the local C.I.D. so I don't have to tell you what that means.
Stacey What does it mean?
Philip (*angrily*) Stacey, for God's sake! Use your imagination! You killed a man! We know you didn't intend to kill him, but nevertheless you killed him!

She turns her back on him and moves to the table. Philip watches her as, with her face averted from him, she thoughtfully picks up the cigarette lighter. Pause

Stacey (*softly, yet unable to conceal the tenseness in her voice*) What is it you want me to do?
Philip You must get in touch with the Inspector. Now, straight away. Tell him you'd like to explain why you left town last night.
Stacey And then what?

Philip (*after a moment, watching her*) Then I suggest you tell me the truth. The whole truth. It's the only way I can help you.

Stacey I've told you the truth. (*Turning, putting down the lighter*) I was attacked and I defended myself.

Philip But you knew the man! You knew Venner!

Stacey Did I?

Philip (*exasperated*) Of course you knew him! If you didn't know him how do you account for the entry in the diary?

Stacey I can't account for it.

Philip And quite apart from the diary, Venner'd just arrived from Paris. He was in Paris whilst you were there.

Stacey (*still the faint trace of defiance in her voice*) Was he?

Philip You know damn well he was!

Stacey hesitates, as if about to say something, then she changes her mind and turns back towards the table. Philip moves to her

Don't you think you'd better tell me about this affair?

Stacey (*annoyed by the tone*) There's nothing to tell.

Philip I want to know exactly what happened on Wednesday.

Stacey I've told you what happened!

Philip What really happened? (*Pause*) Stacey, I warn you—it's not a bit of use being bloody-minded. You're in trouble, serious trouble, and unless you tell me the truth I can't help you.

Stacey (*not looking at him*) I've told you the truth! I'd never set eyes on Venner until he tried to kill me.

Philip I'm sorry. I just don't believe that.

Stacey (*flaring up*) All right—so you don't believe it!

There is a long awkward silence. It is finally broken by the sound of the door buzzer. Philip moves to the window. Pause

Philip (*turning at the window*) There's a police car. It's the Inspector. (*He moves back to Stacey and looks enquiringly at her*) Shall I let him in?

After a momentary hesitation Stacey nods. The door buzzer sounds again

Philip exits

Stacey turns towards the hall. Eventually we hear voices

Philip (*off*) Oh, hello, Inspector.

Lennox (*off*) Is your wife back, sir?

Philip (*off*) Yes, she is.

Philip enters with Lennox

Lennox (*unsmiling*) Good morning, Mrs Harrison.

Stacey Hello, Inspector. (*Conjuring up a friendly smile*) I understand you've been trying to get in touch with me.

Lennox We have. We have indeed, madam.

Stacey I'm afraid I owe you an apology. After you left here yesterday I suddenly took it into my head . . . Oh, do sit down.

Lennox looks at her, but does not move

Would you like some coffee? I was just going to make some . . .
Lennox Thank you. No.
Philip Perhaps I'd better explain about yesterday, Inspector. My wife wasn't feeling too well and she . . .
Lennox (*interrupting him*) I'd rather Mrs Harrison explain. If you've no objection.
Philip No, of course not.

Lennox looks at Stacey

Stacey (*hesitant*) After you left here yesterday morning I was terribly worried and since I wasn't feeling too well I—decided to—go away for a few days. I drove down to Brighton and stayed the night with a friend of mine. This morning—after reading the newspapers—I realized I'd made a mistake and I decided to come back to London.
Lennox I'm glad you did.
Stacey I apologize, Inspector. It was very silly of me dashing away like that without telling anyone. Obviously, it gave you completely the wrong impression.
Lennox Not only me, Mrs Harrison.
Stacey I do assure you, I wasn't running away. I—I was overwrought and tired and I wanted to try and sort things out—in my own mind, as it were . . .
Lennox Yes, well—I'm all for that. I'd be very grateful if you would "sort things out". For instance, yesterday you told me that you'd never heard of Charles Venner; that you'd never seen him before he attacked you.
Stacey Yes, that's right.
Lennox You've no wish to change that statement?
Stacey No, I haven't.
Lennox In spite of the references to you in his diary?

Stacey shakes her head

And in spite of the fact that you were both staying at the same hotel in Paris.
Stacey (*apparently staggered*) The same hotel?
Lennox You did stay at the George Cinq?
Stacey Yes, I did.
Lennox (*nodding*) And so did Mr Venner—for one night. He had a room on the third floor, quite close to yours. He checked in the hotel last Tuesday and left on Wednesday morning—shortly after you, Mrs Harrison.

Philip looks at Stacey

Stacey I—I don't understand. If he did stay at the same hotel it was just a coincidence.

Lennox A coincidence?

Stacey Yes.

Lennox Was it also a coincidence that you both checked out on the same day?

Stacey (*defiantly*) Yes, it was!

Lennox I see.

Philip Do sit down, Inspector.

Lennox hesitates, then moves to an armchair and sits

Lennox Thank you, sir. (*To Stacey*) Well, as it happens I didn't come here just to talk about Mr Venner. I'm interested in yet another friend—or perhaps I should say acquaintance—of yours.

Stacey (*coldly*) Charles Venner was neither a friend of mine nor an acquaintance.

Lennox But Mr Lockwood is, I take it?

Stacey (*surprised*) Peter Lockwood?

Lennox nods

Yes, he's a friend of mine. He's also a client.

Lennox So I understand. How long have you known Mr Lockwood?

Stacey About eight or nine months. He's a friend of my father's.

Philip But why this sudden interest in Peter Lockwood? Had Venner anything to do with the robbery in Eaton Place?

Lennox "Robbery" is hardly the right word, sir, since nothing was stolen.

Stacey (*moving to Lennox; surprised*) Nothing was stolen! But surely the place was ransacked?

Lennox Yes, it was. It was indeed. But nothing was taken away. Certainly nothing of value.

Philip But if nothing was stolen, what was the point of the break-in?

Lennox You tell me, sir. (*Suddenly, turning to Stacey*) Mrs Harrison, did you by any chance telephone Mr Lockwood whilst you were in Paris?

Stacey No.

Lennox You didn't phone him last Tuesday night, for instance, at about half-past nine?

Stacey No, I didn't.

Lennox You're sure?

Stacey (*annoyed*) Of course I'm sure.

Lennox Someone did.

Stacey Well, I didn't!

Lennox According to Mr Lockwood's housekeeper he was upset by the call. Very perturbed, in fact. (*Looking at Stacey*) Also, she seems to think—the housekeeper, that is—that the name Venner was mentioned during the course of the conversation. Not once, apparently, but several times.

Stacey Then I couldn't possibly have made the call, could I, Inspector?

Lennox Why not?

Stacey Because at that time I'd never heard of anyone called Venner!

Lennox gives a little nod and rises

Philip (*quietly*) Have you spoken to Lockwood himself about this?
Lennox Yes. I had a few words with him this morning. (*Not convinced*) He
says the housekeeper was mistaken. The call wasn't from Paris and he's
never heard of Charles Venner!
Stacey But you choose to believe the housekeeper?
Lennox About the phone call, yes. (*Firmly*) You see, we happen to know
that it *was* from Paris, Mrs Harrison.
Stacey (*after a moment*) Well, I'm afraid I can't help you. I didn't make the
call, and I don't know who did.
Lennox Thank you. That's what I wanted to know. (*Turning towards the
hall*) I rather think a colleague of mine—Superintendent Horton—will
want to have a word with you later in the day. I trust you'll be available?
Stacey Yes, I will. Tell the Superintendent if I'm not here, not to panic,
he'll find me at Eaton Place.
Lennox Superintendent Horton doesn't panic very easily, madam.

*Lennox exits. Philip looks at Stacey, then follows the Inspector into the
hall.*
    *Stacey's expression is now serious again. She appears depressed as she
picks up her coat and, after a slight hesitation, goes into the bedroom.*
    *Alan enters from the kitchen. He carries a passport in his hand. He is
obviously surprised to find the room deserted. As he moves towards the sofa
Philip returns*

Alan Where's Stacey?
Philip (*surprised*) She was here a moment ago.
Alan She's probably in her room.
Philip (*noticing the passport*) What's that?
Alan It's her passport. I found it in the car.

Philip goes to him and takes the passport

    (*Puzzled*) It wasn't there on Wednesday, I'm sure of that.

Philip makes no comment. He looks at the passport, turning the pages. Pause

    Stacey enters

    I've put the car away.
Stacey Thank you, Alan. (*She looks at Philip, suddenly realizing that he is
holding her passport*)
Philip Alan found your passport. It was in the car.
Stacey (*hesitantly*) I've been looking for it. I wondered where it was.

*Philip goes to Stacey and hands her the passport. As he does so she avoids
looking at him, turning towards Alan*

Alan It was on the floor, near the passenger seat.
Stacey I must have dropped it getting out of the car. Thank goodness you
found it.

Tiny pause

Alan I'll see you at Peter's.
Stacey Yes, I'll be there in about an hour.

Philip is still looking at Stacey. Alan hesitates, then remembers something and feels in his pocket

Alan Oh, here's the car key.
Stacey Thank you, darling.

As Stacey takes the key, Alan glances at Philip

Alan (*faintly embarrassed, and not quite sure why*) See you later then.
Stacey Yes.
Alan In about an hour . . .

Alan hesitates, then exits

Pause. Stacey stares at the passport, then slowly turning her back on Philip, she crosses and puts it down on the table

Philip Brighton has obviously changed since I was there last. I knew they'd abolished the Belle but I didn't realize you needed your passport.

Pause

Stacey I—I didn't go to Brighton.
Philip No. I rather gathered that. You flew to Paris.
Stacey (*after a slight hesitation*) Yes.
Philip Why? (*Pause*) Why did you go to Paris?
Stacey (*turning*) I went there on business. I tried to do it on the phone but I just couldn't get any sense out of them.
Philip Them?
Stacey The people I'm doing business with.
Philip Who are these people?
Stacey It's—it's a firm called "Doray and Balzac". Their fabrics are fabulous, out of this world, but they're utterly impossible people to deal with. Especially on the telephone.
Philip Why didn't you tell me that you'd been to Paris?
Stacey I don't know. It was very stupid of me. I don't know why I said I'd spent the night in Brighton. (*With almost a vague suggestion of flattery in her voice*) Perhaps because I was a little frightened of you. You probably don't realize it, Philip, but you have a disturbing habit of putting me in the witness-box from time to time.
Philip It's a fault I'm acutely aware of. You have reminded me of it before. However, just as a matter of interest, what are you going to tell the Superintendent when he questions you—as he undoubtedly will—about your visit to Brighton?
Stacey I suppose—I shall have to tell him the truth.
Philip (*acidly*) You suppose you'll have to tell him the truth?
Stacey Yes.
Philip The truth being that you went to Paris?
Stacey Yes.

Philip On business . . .

Stacey Yes.

Philip Well, let's hope he believes you! Because I don't! (*Moving towards her; suddenly angry*) I don't believe a word about this so-called business trip of yours! I think you went to Paris because of Venner . . .

Stacey No!

Philip Because of what happened here, in this room, on Wednesday night!

Stacey (*shaking her head*) That's not true! I've told you why I went there!

Philip (*taking hold of her arm*) Stacey, you've got to tell me the truth!

Stacey I've told you the truth!

Philip I don't believe you! (*Tightening his grip on her arm*) You're lying— and you know damn well you're lying!

Stacey Philip, please!

Philip For God's sake, don't you realize that for once, just once in your life, you're out of your depth!

Stacey Philip, you're hurting me!

He holds her for a moment, then releases her. She feels her arm as she slowly turns away from him

Philip I'm sorry. I didn't mean to hurt you.

An awkward silence

(*Quietly*) You know perfectly well you'll have to tell me the truth sooner or later. You might just as well tell me it now. (*A moment*) Why did you go back to Paris?

Long pause

Stacey I—I had to find something.

Philip What? (*Pause*) What was it you had to find?

Stacey Some—letters . . .

Philip Letters? Letters you'd written?

Stacey Yes.

Philip To whom?

Stacey (*after hesitating*) Venner.

Philip Venner . . .?

Stacey Yes. I—I didn't want the police to get hold of them.

Philip Show me these letters.

Stacey (*surprised by his request*) What?

Philip I said: Show me the letters. Let me see them.

Stacey I can't . . .

Philip Why not?

Stacey I didn't find them.

Philip (*sceptically*) You didn't find them?

Stacey No. I searched his flat from top to bottom but—I just couldn't find them.

Slight pause

Philip Where is this flat?

Stacey It's—it's about fifty kilometres from Paris. At a place called Barbizon.
Philip And you went there last night?
Stacey Yes.
Philip How? How did you go there?
Stacey (*after a moment*) I hired a car . . .
Philip In Paris?
Stacey Yes. At the airport.

Pause

Philip (*quietly, his eyes on her*) Tell me about Venner.

Another pause

Stacey I—I met him about six months ago. In Nice. By coincidence—at least, I think it was a coincidence—we met again, about a fortnight later. (*Pause*) We liked each other, we seemed to have a lot in common, we had mutual friends, so . . . (*She shrugs*)
Philip Go on . . .
Stacey One day, quite by accident, I discovered that he'd been lying to me . . .
Philip About what?
Stacey About his job, his life generally, about—all sorts of things. It was then, and only then I'm afraid, that I realized just how stupid I'd been.
Philip How stupid had you been? (*Pause*) Did he borrow money from you?

Stacey nods

How much?
Stacey About—a thousand pounds, I think.
Philip You think?
Stacey (*faintly harassed*) It didn't matter. It wasn't important. I wasn't worried about the money. I—I iust couldn't get rid of Venner. He wouldn't leave me alone. Wherever I went—theatres, parties, restaurants —he was always there. Always waiting for me.
Philip And on Wednesday?
Stacey You know what happened on Wednesday.
Philip You had a row with him and he tried to kill you?
Stacey (*almost vehemently, with conviction*) No, no! That's not what happened! When he suddenly appeared and grabbed hold of me I thought he was a stranger—someone who'd just broken into the flat. It was only later, after the struggle, after I'd killed him, that I realized who he was.
Philip But didn't he speak to you? Didn't he say something?
Stacey No.
Philip But surely when he got hold of you, when he touched you, you must have recognized him?
Stacey (*shaking her head*) He came from behind the curtain. I had my back to him. I—I was taken completely by surprise.
Philip (*quietly*) I see.

A pause

Stacey Well, that's it. That's it, I'm afraid. Now you know the whole story.

She moves away from him, crossing down towards the cigarette box on the table. As she opens the box and takes out a cigarette she suddenly becomes acutely aware of the fact that he is still staring at her. There is a defiant look on her face as she slowly turns and faces him again. Pause

Stacey Don't you believe me? Don't you believe what I've told you?

Philip (*slowly*) I don't know, Stacey. I don't know whether to believe you or not.

CURTAIN

ACT II
SCENE 1

The same. Several hours later. Friday evening

Alan is kneeling by the side of the record-player, searching through a pile of records for a particular LP. He is only partly dressed and looks both worried and annoyed as he fails to find the LP he is looking for. Finally he rises and stands for a moment staring down at the pile of records, then a sudden thought occurs to him and he turns and hurries into the bedroom. Pause. The door buzzer is heard. Pause. The buzzer sounds again

Alan rushes back into the room, carrying an LP (his birthday present to Brad) at the same time struggling into a dressing-gown. He crosses to the record-player, hesitates, then as the buzzer sounds again turns and looks towards the hall. Another pause. The door buzzer sounds again. Almost as if alerted by the buzzer Alan suddenly takes the LP out of its sleeve and puts it on the record-player. He then carefully places the sleeve under a pile of records and goes into the hall. Pause. Alan returns with Brad

Alan Why didn't you use your key?

Brad (*tired*) Because I forgot my flaming keys, that's why! (*Relenting*) I'm sorry Alan. I've had a pretty tiring day.

Alan Me, too. I've been at Eaton Place since eleven o'clock this morning and, quite apart from Stacey being in a filthy mood, every damn thing that could go wrong has gone wrong! Even the curtain people have taken leave of their senses! (*Indicating a large roll of curtain material in the hall*) I found that outside the front door and it should have been delivered to Peter's.

Brad (*sitting on the sofa*) Where is Stacey? Is she still at Peter's?

Alan Yes, and the way things are going it looks as if she'll be there all night! But how are you, Brad? I hear you've got an ulcer.

Brad Bad news travels fast. How did you know?

Alan I was with Stacey when you telephoned her. No more booze, I take it?

Brad You take it right! It's milk from now on, I'm afraid. And I hate the stuff. I really do, Alan. I even hate the adverts. All that pinta nonsense!

Alan What sort of an ulcer is it?

Brad I don't know. I didn't ask them.

Alan You didn't ask them?! If it had been me I'd have asked that many questions the doc would have torn his hair out.

Brad I doubt it. This doctor was a pretty little blonde.

The door buzzer sounds

Alan See who that is, Brad.

Alan exits to the bedroom.
Brad, somewhat reluctantly, rises and goes out to the hall. He returns
with Gerald Waddington. Gerald is wearing a dinner-jacket and carries an
overcoat

Brad I'm awfully sorry, Stacey's not here. She's at Peter Lockwood's.

Gerald (*concerned*) What time are you expecting her back?

Brad I don't know. It's difficult to say. Is there anything I can do?

Gerald I've arranged to take Stacey out to dinner on Sunday and it looks
as if I shall have to cancel it.

Brad All right, I'll tell her.

Gerald It's damned annoying, I was really looking forward to it! I've got
to go to Brussels and I doubt whether I'll be back in time.

Brad Don't worry, I'll see she gets the message. What's happening in
Brussels, Gerald? Are you buying up the Grand Place?

Gerald The last time I had lunch there I thought I had bought it.

Brad I can imagine! I'll tell Stacey you called.

Gerald nods, half turns towards the hall, then hesitates

Gerald I'm—very worried, Brad. About Stace, I mean.

Brad Yes, I know. We all are.

Gerald I don't think she quite realizes just how serious this Venner
business is.

Brad I think she does. But unfortunately there's nothing she can do about
it.

Gerald (*hesitantly*) Except, perhaps, tell the truth.

Brad (*somewhat surprised by this remark*) Are you suggesting that she
hasn't told the truth?

Gerald (*faintly on edge*) I don't know. I just feel that somehow . . .
(*Putting down his coat*) Do you know a man called Lennox?

Brad Yes. He's a police Inspector.

Gerald He telephoned me this morning, just after I left here. He said he
knew I was a friend of Stacey's and he wondered if, by any chance, I
was also a friend of Charles Venner's.

Brad What did you say?

Gerald I said I wasn't a friend of Venner's and so far as I knew neither
was Stace.

Brad Thank you, Gerald. I'm glad you said that.

Gerald Yes, but—I don't know whether he believed me or not.

Brad Why shouldn't he believe you?

Gerald About a week ago I popped over to Paris for the day. A friend of
mine's just opened a dress shop on the Left Bank and since I helped to
finance the venture I thought I'd better find out what she was up to.
Anyway, I took the opportunity of taking Stace out to lunch.

Brad She told me.

Gerald She was staying at the George Cinq and we arranged to meet in the
cocktail bar. Just as I arrived she came down in the lift. There was one
other person in the lift besides Stace. It was Venner.

Brad Venner! Are you sure?
Gerald I'm absolutely sure. I saw his picture in one of the newspapers and recognised him immediately.

Pause

Brad Have you spoken to Stacey about this?
Gerald Yes.
Brad What did she say?
Gerald (*after a slight hesitation*) She doesn't recall the incident.
Brad You mean, she doesn't want to know?

Gerald nods. Slight pause

Gerald I don't have to tell you what would have happened if I'd opened my big mouth and told the Inspector about this.
Brad (*looking at him*) But you didn't?
Gerald No, of course I didn't! But it isn't to say he's not going to find out about it. (*Pause*) Brad, I hate to say this, but I think Stace is taking a risk—a very big risk—by not being completely frank about all this . . .
Brad I couldn't agree with you more. And I wish you'd tell her that.
Gerald Yes—well, I might do just that. (*He looks at his watch*) I'm not due at the Savoy till eight o'clock. You say she's at Peter Lockwood's.
Brad Yes. It's only just round the corner, in Eaton Place. Why not drop in on her?
Gerald Thank you. I'll probably do that. (*He picks up his coat and is about to leave*)
Brad Gerald, wait a minute! Before you go. There's something I want to ask you. (*Pause*) What do you think happened on Wednesday night?
Gerald (*after a moment*) Surely, we know what happened, Venner attacked Stacey, there was a struggle, and he was killed.
Brad Yes, I know, but . . . (*He hesitates, looks at Gerald*)
Gerald Do you want me to tell you what I really think?
Brad Yes, I do.
Gerald (*after a moment*) I think Stace had been having an affair with Venner and was trying to break it off. It's my bet she'd been trying to ditch him for some time and he just wouldn't wear it. In the end the little bastard got difficult, lost his temper, and tried to kill her.
Brad (*quietly*) I see.
Gerald I'm sorry, Brad—but that's what I really think.
Brad And what's going to happen now?
Gerald I don't know. You tell me. But one thing I do know. She's got to tell this chap Lennox the truth, the whole truth, because if she doesn't— (*shaking his head*) God only knows what will happen!

As Brad gives a worried little nod of agreement the telephone rings

Gerald Take care of yourself, Brad.
Brad (*moving to the phone*) Thank you, Gerald.

Gerald exits

Brad (*on the phone*) Five-eight-nine seven-eight-four-three . . . Hello?
. . . Hello! . . . (*Pause*) I'm sorry, you'll have to speak up, I can't hear
you . . . (*Pause*) Hello . . . I can't hear you! . . .

*Alan enters. He is now dressed, except for a jacket, but is obviously having
trouble with the strap on his wrist*

Alan Who is it?
Brad I don't know. It sounds like someone in a call-box. (*He replaces the
receiver*)
Alan Brad, tighten this damn thing for me, will you?

Brad goes to Alan and, taking hold of his wrist, proceeds to tighten the strap

Brad Are you on that skiing lark again tonight?
Alan Yes.
Brad Well, watch out for that chair.
Alan Very funny.

Pause

Brad How's that?
Alan That's fine. Thank you.
Brad (*releasing his wrist*) I've just been talking to Gerald Waddington.
Alan Yes, I know. I heard you.

Brad looks at him, surprised

I always listen to what Gerald Waddington's got to say. (*Returning to
the bedroom*) You never know what useful information you might pick
up.

Alan exits

*The telephone rings. Brad goes and lifts the receiver, his thoughts still with
Alan*

Brad Five-eight-nine seven-eight-four-three . . . Hello? . . . Yes, speaking . . . (*Astonished, taken completely by surprise*) Dominic! . . .
Where are you? . . . Where are you speaking from? . . . But why on
earth didn't you tell me you were coming. I'd have met you at the airport!
. . . No, of course not . . . (*Pause*) Yes, I'm listening . . . (*Tensely,
with a glance towards the bedroom*) Wait a minute! We can't talk now!
Give me your number and I'll call you back . . . (*with a note of
desperation*) Don't argue, give me the number! . . . (*Scribbling on a pad*)
I'll ring you from a call-box . . . in five minutes, it's just round the
corner! (*Cutting him short*) Dominic, do as I tell you! Stay where you
are—I'll ring you back!

*Brad replaces the receiver, tears the note off the pad, and with an anxious
glance in the direction of the bedroom crosses towards the hall. He freezes.
Someone is obviously unlocking the front door and is about to enter the flat*

Brad hesitates, then quickly turns and goes out to the kitchen. The back door is heard to open and close.
After a slight pause Stacey enters from the hall. She looks distinctly tired. As she slowly takes off her things she stares at the curtain material in the hall.
Alan enters. He is now wearing a ski jacket and carrying a pair of gloves

Stacey (*indicating the curtain material*) Alan, what on earth is this doing here?
Alan I found it outside the front door. They delivered it here by mistake.
Stacey Really! The idiots! Lance has been waiting for this since three o'clock this afternoon!
Alan Yes, I know. I'll drop it in on him.
Stacey There's no need, darling. I'll take it. I've got to go back later. My God, what a frustrating day! (*Turning*) Where's Brad? Have you seen him?
Alan (*puzzled*) He was here a few minutes ago. He must have slipped out for something.
Stacey How does he seem?

Alan hesitates

Alan Since you ask me, I—think he's very worried, Stacey.
Stacey (*surprised*) He didn't sound worried when he spoke to me on the phone.
Alan No, I know he didn't. He obviously didn't want to upset you.
Stacey What makes you think he's worried? Has he said anything about this afternoon? About the X-rays?
Alan No, not a thing, it's just that . . . Now, look—don't misunderstand me! He looks all right and he appears to be as cheerful as ever. It's just that, personally, I can't help feeling that. . . . (*He hesitates*)
Stacey Can't help feeling what, Alan?
Alan Well—I can't help feeling that, in spite of how he talks, he's really very, very worried. But I could be wrong, Stacey! After all, I don't know Brad all that well. (*Indicating the curtain material*) Now are you sure you don't want me to drop that in for you? I shall be going past Peter's.
Stacey No, darling, I'll see to it.

Alan exits

After a pause, Stacey thoughtfully picks up her things and is about to go into the bedroom when voices are heard from the hall. She looks towards it

Philip (*off*) Hello, Alan. Is Stacey in?
Alan (*off*) Yes, she's just got back. Go along in.
Stacey Hello, Philip!
Philip (*quietly, unsmiling*) How long have you been here?
Stacey I've just arrived. I've been at Eaton Place all day. And what a day! Why does everything take so confoundedly long in this country?

Philip Not everything. (*Tiny pause*) Have you seen the Inspector?
Stacey Not since you were here this morning.
Philip The police haven't been in touch with you?
Stacey No, why? (*As Philip hesitates*) You've heard something?
Philip (*after a moment*) Yes—I've heard something.
Stacey What is it?
Philip (*after another hesitation*) I think they're going to arrest you, Stacey.
Stacey Arrest me? On what charge?
Philip Murder.
Stacey (*angrily*) But that's ridiculous! It's absurd! They can't do that!
Philip I'm afraid they can.
Stacey But it wasn't murder! The police know what happened!
Philip (*quietly*) You knew Venner. You'd had an affair with him.
Stacey (*flaring up*) Whether I knew him or not is beside the point! You
know perfectly well that if I hadn't picked up that knife . . .
Philip (*stopping her*) Stacey! (*After a pause; quietly*) If I'm going to help
you—and God knows you're going to need help—you've just got to stop
blowing your top and start listening to what I've got to say!
Stacey (*interrupting*) I am not blowing my top!
Philip (*fiercely*) Do you want me to help you, or don't you want me to
help you? Now make your mind up!

Stacey is obviously taken aback by the sudden note of authority in his voice

Stacey (*after a pause*) If what you say is true, I haven't much choice, have
I?
Philip No, you haven't much choice. (*Tiny pause*) When the Inspector
arrives I want you to answer his questions, but say as little as possible.
Is that clear?
Stacey (*softly*) Yes . . .
Philip Later—after they've charged you—I'll tell Lennox about the letters,
about renting the Renault, about you going out to Barbizon. But I don't
want him to hear that story now. Not tonight. You understand?
Stacey Yes, I understand.
Philip (*quietly*) Now, is there anything else you want to tell me? Anything
you've forgotten?
Stacey No.
Philip You're quite sure?
Stacey Yes, I'm quite sure. But how did you know about the Renault? I
simply told you I'd rented a car. I didn't say what it was.
Philip After I left you this morning I made it my job to find out whether
your story was true or not. You've told me so many lies I just had to
make sure that this time you really were telling me the truth! I telephoned
Orly airport and spoke to the Hertz people. They confirmed your story.

*As Philip finishes speaking the door buzzer is heard. They both look towards
the hall. Pause*

If that's Lennox—remember what I've just told you!

Stacey hesitates, then with a nod of the head she goes out into the hall

*Philip watches the hall, an anxious expression on his face. Eventually voices
are heard*

Lennox (*off*) Good evening, Mrs Harrison. May I come in?
Stacey (*off*) Yes, of course, Inspector. Please do . . .

Stacey returns with Lennox. The Inspector is carrying his briefcase

Philip Good evening, Inspector.
Lennox Good evening to you, sir. I was hoping you'd be here. I called on
you earlier this evening but unfortunately we just missed each other.
Philip (*puzzled*) You wanted to see me, Inspector?
Lennox Yes. I've got something I'd like to show you.

*Lennox moves to the sofa, opens his briefcase, and takes out a postcard-size
photograph*

Would you and Mrs Harrison kindly take a look at this photograph?

As Stacey moves down to the sofa Lennox hands her the photograph. Pause

Do you know that woman?
Stacey (*staring at the photograph, puzzled*) No.
Lennox You've never seen her before?
Stacey No, I haven't.

Philip moves to Stacey

Lennox (*carefully, watching her*) You're sure, Mrs Harrison?
Stacey (*bewildered*) Yes, I'm quite sure.

Lennox nods, obviously believing her. Philip takes the photograph from her

Philip (*looking at the photograph*) Who is she?
Lennox Which means you don't know the lady either, sir?
Philip No, I don't. Should I know her?
Lennox (*pleasantly*) That's for you to tell me, sir.
Philip I've never seen her before.
Lennox You're positive—quite positive about that?
Philip I couldn't be more positive, Inspector.
Lennox (*obviously satisfied*) Thank you, sir.

Tiny pause

Philip (*a shade irritated*) Well, since you've obviously succeeded in arous-
ing our curiosity, perhaps now you'll satisfy it. Who is she?
Lennox Her name is Joanna Mansfield. About two years ago she was
arrested for theft and given a suspended sentence. (*Taking the photograph
out of Philip's hand*) At the present moment she's a chambermaid at a
hotel in Bloomsbury. (*As he returns the photograph to his briefcase*) The
Winston Hotel.

Philip The Winston? That's where Venner was staying!
Lennox That's right, sir.

As Stacey moves to the armchair she nods towards the sofa. Lennox acknowledges the gesture, and sits down

Miss Mansfield came to see me this afternoon. She walked into my office and made a statement which, to say the least, was something of a bombshell.
Philip (*puzzled*) What did she say.
Lennox Well, the first thing she said was: "Inspector, if you think Stacey Harrison was having an affair with Charles Venner—you're very much mistaken." (*To Stacey*) She then went on to say that you'd never seen Venner, never set eyes on him, until Wednesday evening—and what's more she could prove it! (*Quietly, closing his briefcase*) After that, she told me her story. (*Pause*) She said that on Wednesday night, shortly after Venner was killed, she was paid a hundred pounds simply to place a diary—the one I showed you, Mrs Harrison—in the pocket of a jacket belonging to the dead man.
Philip Good God!
Stacey Did she tell you who paid her the hundred pounds?
Lennox She claims that a man telephoned her at the hotel and said that he was a friend of a friend of hers and that he had a proposition that might interest her. They met late on Wednesday night. He gave her the diary and there and then handed over the money.
Philip Did she say who the man was?
Lennox No. Only that he was a stranger to her.
Philip Didn't she describe him?
Lennox No; she flatly refused to describe him, or tell us anything about him. She wouldn't even tell us where they'd met.
Philip (*sceptically*) And you believed this story?
Lennox No, sir. I didn't . . .
Philip Then what on earth . . .
Lennox (*stopping him*) Not at first! But I believe it now! You see, on investigation we found Miss Mansfield's fingerprints not only on the plastic coathanger belonging to the sports jacket, but on the actual diary itself. Also, we've now compared the handwriting in the diary with a letter that Venner wrote to the hotel. (*Shaking his head*) It's not the same.
Philip (*incredulously*) You mean—she really was telling the truth?
Lennox Yes, sir. There's no doubt about it! No doubt about it whatsoever!

Philip turns and stares at Stacey in utter bewilderment. She stares back at him. Then suddenly she starts laughing. There is almost a note of hysteria in her laughter. Lennox is quick to detect this and he glances anxiously across at Philip. As Stacey's laughter continues to get even more hysterical Philip moves towards her. Lennox rises

Philip Stop it, Stacey! Stop it!

Finally, in desperation, Philip grabs hold of Stacey by the shoulders and

violently shakes her in an attempt to stop the hysteria. Pause. As Stacey
slowly recovers, she moves to Lennox

Stacey I'm sorry. I'm sorry, Inspector . . .

Pause

Philip (*concerned, offering her his handkerchief*) Are you all right now?
Stacey (*with a little nod*) Yes. I—I really don't know what got into me. (*To Lennox*) I'm terribly sorry.
Lennox Not to worry, Mrs Harrison.
Philip Why do you think she decided to tell you this story, Inspector?
Lennox She said she came to see me because, after reading the newspapers and learning that Venner had been killed, she was frightened.
Stacey Frightened?
Lennox (*nodding*) She said the papers had suddenly brought home to her the fact that she'd been responsible, or at any rate partly responsible for throwing suspicion on to an innocent person.
Philip In other words, she had a guilty conscience?
Lennox Yes.
Philip And you believe that?
Lennox (*after a slight pause*) Yes, I do. So far as I can see, it's the only possible explanation. Mrs Harrison, has anyone a particular grudge against you at the moment? Have you quarrelled with anyone just recently?
Stacey No, I don't think so.
Lennox You can't think of anyone who would deliberately try to incriminate you like this?
Stacey No, I can't. It's quite beyond my comprehension.

Lennox hesitates

Lennox Mrs Harrison, in spite of what Miss Mansfield told me, one curious fact still remains. Venner *was* in Paris whilst you were there. He did stay at the same hotel, if only for one night.
Stacey If that's true, I certainly don't remember seeing him.
Lennox (*friendly*) You really think it was just a coincidence, that he was staying at the same hotel?
Stacey I don't know. I don't know whether it was a coincidence or not.
Lennox (*still quite friendly*) How long were you in Paris?
Stacey About three weeks.
Lennox Did you buy anything whilst you were there?
Stacey (*puzzled*) Yes, I did. I bought myself a bracelet and a trouser suit . . .
Lennox (*quietly, looking at her*) Didn't you buy a painting?
Stacey No.
Lennox But surely, you brought one back with you?
Stacey Yes, that's quite right. I did. But it was a birthday present for my father.
Lennox From an ex-pupil of his—a man called Dominic?
Stacey (*surprised*) Why, yes!

Lennox How did you get the picture? Was it delivered to the hotel, or did you go out to Barbizon for it?
Philip (*completely taken aback*) Barbizon?
Lennox (*turning towards Philip curiously*) Yes, sir?
Philip But why Barbizon?
Lennox That's where Dominic lives; where he has his studio.
Philip (*after a moment; looking at Stacey*) Oh. Oh, I see.
Stacey (*not looking at Philip, but acutely aware of the fact that he is staring at her*) The picture was delivered to the hotel the day I left. Just as I was driving away, in fact.
Lennox (*obviously interested in this statement*) Just as you were driving away?
Stacey Yes.

Tiny pause

Lennox Was this the first time you'd delivered a picture to your father?
Stacey . . . Yes.
Lennox But surely, unless I'm mistaken, he's received other pictures from Dominic?
Stacey Yes, he has.
Lennox But you didn't deliver them to him?
Stacey No, I didn't.
Lennox (*on the verge of asking her yet another question, then changing his mind*) Thank you, Mrs Harrison. Thank you, sir. I won't take up any more of your time.

Lennox picks up his briefcase and goes out into the hall. Stacey glances nervously at Philip, then follows the Inspector

Pause. We hear the closing of the front door. Philip looks both puzzled and angry as he watches the hall, waiting for Stacey to return

Stacey enters

Philip Why did you go to Paris—to Barbizon?

Stacey does not answer him, instead she moves slowly down to the writing table

Was it to see Dominic?
Stacey Yes.
Philip Then that story you told me—about the letters, about Venner making a nuisance of himself . . .
Stacey (*tensely*) It wasn't true! I made it up!
Philip (*incredulously*) You made it up!
Stacey (*with a note of defiance*) Yes!
Philip Just like that, on the spur of the moment?
Stacey Yes!
Philip But why? Why in God's name do a thing like that?

Stacey Because I knew you wouldn't believe me if I told you the truth, that's why!

Philip Why wouldn't I believe you?

Stacey Because I tried it once before when I told you about Stockholm and I wasn't exactly successful! Remember?

Philip (*intensely angry*) Stacey, why did you lie to me? Why did you tell me that story?

Stacey I've told you why!

Philip (*shaking his head*) No, no. You had another reason! (*Moving to her; even angrier than before*) You must have had another reason! What was it, Stacey?

Long pause

Stacey (*softly*) I—I didn't want you to find out about Brad . . .

Philip Brad?

Stacey Yes. And the telegram . . .

Philip (*puzzled*) Telegram? Which telegram?

Stacey The one that arrived on Wednesday, just before Venner appeared. (*She opens a drawer in the writing table and takes out a telegram*) I found it in my dressing-gown pocket yesterday morning, after you and the Inspector had left. I was so upset I didn't realize it was for Brad until I'd opened it. (*She pauses, then reads the telegram*) "Man called Charles Venner arriving London. Under no circumstances talk to him. Dominic."

Philip slowly takes the telegram from her and looks at it. Pause

Stacey Now you know why I really went back to Paris. I wanted to ask Dominic about the telegram. To try and find out what he and Brad were up to.

Philip (*quietly, looking at her*) And did you?

Stacey No. When I got to the studio it was completely deserted. I waited the best part of four hours, but no-one turned up, nothing happened. In the end I drove back to the airport.

Philip stares at her for a moment, then looks at the telegram again. Pause

Philip Has Brad seen this?

Stacey shakes her head

You didn't show it to him?

Stacey No, I didn't.

Philip Why not? I should have thought the first thing you'd have done was show Brad the telegram and ask him what it was all about.

Stacey (*nodding*) I nearly did that. And then, at the very last moment, I changed my mind. I don't know why, but I thought if I could get Dominic to tell me his side of the story first Brad would be more likely to confide in me.

Philip Does he know you've tried to see Dominic?

Stacey No, I've only spoken to him for a few minutes. That was this

morning just as I arrived home. He was on his way to the hospital.
Philip And you said nothing?
Stacey No. Your mother was with him. I didn't want to get Madge
involved.
Philip (*after a pause*) That picture—the one you brought back from Paris,
the one the Inspector mentioned . . .
Stacey Yes?
Philip What's it like?
Stacey It's terrible! Just awful!
Philip Does Brad think it's terrible?
Stacey Yes—we both do. That's what I don't understand. I can't imagine
why the police are interested in it. But judge for yourself.

Stacey goes into the bedroom

Philip moves down to the sofa, looking at the telegram. Pause

*Stacey returns carrying the "sack" containing the picture. She props the
"sack" against the sofa and makes an attempt to open it. It is then that she
realizes that the "sack" has recently been fastened by a strand of wire*

Stacey (*trying to unfasten the wire*) What on earth . . .
Philip Let me help you . . . (*He struggles with the wire*)
Stacey This wire's new; it wasn't there originally.

*Philip finally removes the strand of wire and as he does so the "sack" drops
to the floor revealing the picture. Stacey stares at the painting in amazement.
It is a Raoul Dufy water colour. (Piazetta Di San Marco, Venice, 1938)*

Stacey This isn't the same picture!
Philip I gathered that. (*Pause*) It's a Dufy . . .
Stacey Yes. (*Bewildered*) I don't understand! Where's the other picture?
What's happened to the other painting? (*Staring at the picture*) Is this
an original Dufy?
Philip Well—it certainly looks like it. (*Pointing*) It's signed. (*Tiny pause*)
Stacey, how well off is Brad?
Stacey He's not well off at all. He certainly couldn't afford to buy a picture
like this, if that's what you're thinking.
Philip (*shaking his head*) No, that's not what I was thinking.
Stacey He's got a little money in the bank, perhaps two or three thousand,
and he's got a pension, of course, which is about seventeen hundred a
year.
Philip And that's it?
Stacey Yes. Of course, he gambles a lot, especially at cards, and he's ter-
ribly lucky. (*Hesitantly*) At least, he says he is.
Philip (*looking at her*) Have you ever played cards with him?
Stacey No.
Philip Neither have I! And neither have any of our friends so far as I can
make out! (*Looking at the picture again*) If this isn't a Dufy, it's a very

good fake. In which case, what's Brad doing with it? And where did he get it from?

Stacey We know where he got it from. He got it from Dominic.

Philip Could Dominic have painted it?

Stacey Good heavens, no! (*Pause*) Although, come to think of it, he used to paint some wonderful pictures. Then suddenly, for no apparent reason at all, his work just deteriorated. It was almost as if . . . (*She hesitates*)

Philip What are you suggesting? That Dominic deliberately turned out hack work as a cover-up for—this sort of thing?

Stacey I think that's possible, don't you?

Philip (*thoughtfully*) Yes, I do.

Stacey (*looking at the picture*) We could be wrong, of course. It may not be a fake . . .

Philip Yes. Well—I think the first thing we'd better do is find out whether it is. Now how do we go about that?

Stacey I have a friend at the Tate. I haven't seen him for ages but I dare say . . . (*She stops: a sudden thought has occurred to her*) I know! I could take it to the Clinic and let Peter have a look at it.

Philip Peter Lockwood? I'm not sure that's a good idea. He's a friend of Brad's. (*He looks at her*) Would he know whether it was genuine?

Stacey Yes. He'd know immediately.

Pause. Philip is giving the suggestion careful thought

Philip All right, you do that. I'll stay here and tackle your father. (*Picking up the picture*) But don't say too much to Peter, just show him the picture and ask him whether it's genuine or not. I'll meet you later at the Clinic.

Stacey (*obviously hesitating*) Yes, all right.

Philip I'll take the picture down to the car for you.

Philip is aware of her hesitation

What is it?

Stacey Please—don't be too tough on Brad.

Philip I'll simply listen to what he's got to say, Stacey.

Stacey gives a worried little nod and picking up her coat and scarf exits, followed by Philip

Pause

There is the sound of the back door opening and closing and then Brad enters from the kitchen and crosses down to the sofa. He appears a weary and very worried man as he stands by the sofa staring into space

Pause. Suddenly he feels a slight pain coming on and for a moment he holds on to the back of the sofa for support. Pause. Gradually the ulcer pain subsides and with a little sigh of relief Brad slowly straightens himself. Another pause. He looks at his watch, hesitates, then almost as if he has reached a sudden decision he goes to the phone, and starts to dial

Philip enters from the hall

Brad stares at him in amazement as he puts down the phone

Brad Philip! I was just about to phone you . . .
Philip (*quietly*) Were you, Brad?
Brad Yes. I—I wanted to ask your advice about—something. (*After a moment; nervously*) Where's Stacey?
Philip She's gone to see Peter Lockwood. What is it you wanted to ask me?
Brad I'm in trouble, Philip. Serious trouble, I'm afraid.
Philip Yes, I know.

Brad looks at him

We found the picture.
Brad The picture?
Philip The Dufy.
Brad Oh . . . (*Pause*) It's not a Dufy. It's a fake. It was painted by a man called Dominic. (*Another pause*) I expect you've heard of him?
Philip Yes, I've heard of him.
Brad That's—what I wanted to talk to you about.
Philip (*a shade unfriendly*) All right, Brad. Go ahead.

Pause. Brad hesitates, then moves to the sofa and sits

Brad Dominic used to be a pupil of mine. Just over four years ago he went to live in Paris. After he'd been there about six months he invited me to spend a week-end with him. He said he'd just finished painting a picture and he particularly wanted me to see it. I arrived at his studio on a Friday night, but he didn't show me the painting until the day I was leaving. And then, to my amazement, he produced a perfect copy of a Matisse. It was so perfect I just couldn't believe that Dominic had painted it! Well, to cut a long story short—I was so intrigued by the picture I asked Dominic if I could bring it back to London with me.
Philip Why?
Brad I wanted to show it to Peter Lockwood, I don't know whether you've met Peter . . .
Philip No, but I've heard a great deal about him.
Brad He's an odd sort of chap. Very kind—extraordinarily kind at times—but he has a wicked sense of humour. It usually consists of getting the better of people. Anyway, I showed Peter the painting and his reaction was exactly what I expected. He was astonished; he just couldn't believe it was a fake. Rather to my surprise he asked if he could borrow the picture for a few days and I said, yes of course, why not? About a week later he telephoned me and I went round to see him. (*Slight pause*) It was then that he told me that he'd sold the painting to an art dealer—a man he disliked intensely—for twelve thousand pounds.
Philip You mean—he'd sold it as an original, as a Matisse?
Brad Yes.
Philip (*quietly*) And what happened to the money, the twelve thousand?

Brad He gave it to me.
Philip And you kept it?
Brad No. I gave Dominic seven thousand, I sent three thousand to a pet charity of mine, anonymously—and I —kept the rest.
Philip You kept two thousand pounds?
Brad Yes.
Philip Only two thousand?
Brad You don't believe me?
Philip (*after a moment*) Yes, I believe you, Brad.
Brad Later—apart from the Matisse—we received a Picasso and two Utrillos.
Philip Fakes?

Brad nods

All painted by Dominic?
Brad Yes.
Philip What happened to them?
Brad Peter sold them.
Philip To dealers?
Brad Yes, always dealers. Peter hates dealers—positively loathes them. (*Slight pause*) It was after we'd sold the Utrillos that I started to get worried. I think we both felt that we were beginning to get hooked on the operation. Gently hooked, perhaps, but nevertheless hooked. Anyway, we agreed to call it a day, so I contacted Dominic and arranged a meeting. And that's when the trouble started!
Philip Dominic wasn't prepared to call it a day?
Brad Definitely not! He was quite frank about it. He said he just couldn't afford to pack it in. Not only that, he said we'd only disposed of four pictures in three years—which was true—and he could turn out fakes, first class forgeries, at the rate of one a month. One every two weeks if necessary.
Philip Was he telling the truth?
Brad Yes, I think he was. Anyway, we argued the toss for about an hour and finally I agreed that we'd dispose of one more picture. The Dufy— the one Stacey brought back.
Philip Go on, Brad.
Brad Then—about a week ago—I had a letter from Dominic. He said that someone—he didn't mention who—had found out about the forgeries and was trying to blackmail him. And what's more this man was very anxious to meet me too! I didn't like the sound of this, and neither did Peter. In the end, I decided to ignore the letter. I wish now I hadn't. The man he referred to was Venner.
Philip Venner? Are you sure it was Venner?
Brad Yes. Dominic told me it was.
Philip When did you speak to Dominic?
Brad About five minutes ago. He telephoned me from Heathrow, having just arrived from Paris. The funny thing is he swears blue he sent me a telegram about Venner. If he did, I never received it.

Philip What else did Dominic tell you?

Brad He's teamed up with someone else, someone here, in London. The man who threw suspicion on to Stacey.

Philip Who is this new partner of Dominic's, do you know?

Brad No, I don't, but as I understand it he's going to contact me later this evening. But Dominic says not to worry, everythings going to be all right. (*Grimly*) Always providing of course I keep my mouth shut.

Philip Did you ask him what would happen to you if you didn't keep your mouth shut?

Brad (*rising*) Yes, I did. He said: "Poor old Peter didn't keep his mouth shut. And you know what happened to him!" (*Pause*) Philip, I know I've broken the law, I know I've been stupid, but—well, the fact is I'm out of my depth and I just don't know what to do about it.

Philip looks at his father-in-law for a moment, then reaches a decision

Philip All right, Brad, I'll try and help you—but from what you've told me so far, it's not going to be easy. Be in my Chambers tomorrow morning at twelve o'clock.

Brad Thank you, Philip. I'll be there—and I'm very grateful.

Philip Don't be too grateful. You may not like my advice when you get it.

Exit Philip

Brad stands thoughtfully looking towards the hall, finally crossing down to the drinks trolley. Hardly aware of his movements, he picks up an unopened bottle of Scotch and slowly opens it. Gradually it dawns on him what he is doing and, realizing that he is now forbidden alcohol, he replaces the bottle

Brad exits to the kitchen

After a moment the telephone rings—and continues to ring

Brad hurries back into the room and crosses to the phone. He has obviously been eating a biscuit in the kitchen and the remainder of it is still in his hand

Brad (*on the phone*) . . . Just hold on, I'm in the kitchen. I've got some milk on the stove!

Brad puts the receiver down on the table and returns to the kitchen

Long pause

Alan slowly enters from the hall. He is now wearing the pair of gloves. His manner is tense and cautious as he takes stock of the room, his eyes eventually coming to rest on the record-player. With a final glance towards the bedroom and the kitchen he swiftly crosses down to the record-player and switches it on

Music. A tiny pause—then Alan quite deliberately turns up the sound and the music swells into the room

In a matter of seconds an astonished Brad appears from the kitchen; a glass of hot milk in his hand. He stares across at the record-player in utter amazement. Puzzled, he puts down the glass of milk, and is crossing to the record-player when he sees Alan

(*Astonished*) I thought you were having a lesson!

Alan quickly draws a gun from the pocket of his ski jacket and fires it at Brad. Brad reels back, finally collapsing across the nearby armchair. Alan stares at the body for a brief moment, then quickly gets to work—intent on making Brad's murder appear as suicide. He moves the body into the chair; carefully arranging it so that it would appear that the dead man had slumped forward after shooting himself. When he is finally satisfied with the position of the body he places the gun in Brad's hand, carefully establishing the dead man's finger-prints on the murder weapon. He now stands back and surveys the body, making sure that he has not overlooked anything. As he glances up he notices the glass of milk and hesitates, undecided whether to dispose of it or not. After a moment he moves down to the table and is about to pick up the glass when, once again, he hesitates. As he glances towards the kitchen it is obvious that he is still un-decided whether to empty the glass or leave it untouched. Finally, he decides to leave the glass of milk where it is, and turns his attention towards the record-player. It is then, and only then, that he notices that the telephone receiver is off. He stops dead, staring at the receiver on the table. Obviously puzzled, he crosses to the table and carefully picks up the phone. For a brief moment it looks as if he is going to put the receiver to his ear, then he changes his mind, replaces it, and rushes quickly out into the hall

Alan exits, and the front door is heard to slam

The music continues from the record-player. After a moment the telephone starts to ring again. It continues to ring, as—

the Lights fade to a Black-out

SCENE 2

The same. Late Saturday morning

The room is deserted, but Alan's suitcase and valise are on the floor near the sofa. Madge enters from the kitchen carrying a tray of coffee and sandwiches. Although she is obviously depressed there is an air of authority about her; she gives the impression of being temporarily in charge of the flat. As Madge crosses the room there is the sound of the front door opening, then Alan appears. He is wearing an overcoat and scarf

Madge (*as she puts down the tray*) Did you manage to find a taxi?
Alan Yes, I was lucky, there was one on the stand. I'll be off then, Madge.
(*Moving to the suitcase*) Say good-bye to Philip for me. And if Stacey
takes a turn for the better and would like to see me, I'll be at Peter
Lockwood's. I'm not going home until this evening.
Madge Yes, all right, But my guess is, she won't want to see anyone.
(*Concerned*) I'm getting quite worried about her. I really am.
Alan Well—if you'd like me to stay . . .
Madge No. No, there's no need. There's nothing you can do. I've made
some sandwiches, but I doubt whether she'll even look at them! She's
had absolutely nothing to eat all day.

Philip enters from the bedroom. He looks tired and concerned

Philip (*to Alan*) Are you off?
Alan Yes, I'm just going. If Stacey wants to get in touch with me, or you
for that matter, I'll be at Eaton Place. I shan't be going back to Dedham
until this evening.
Philip Yes, all right, Alan.
Alan Now, please, let me know if there's anything I can do. Don't hesitate.

Philip gives a thoughtful little nod

Alan picks up his belongings and exits

Madge turns towards the tray

Madge I've made some coffee and sandwiches.

Philip makes no comment. He looks distinctly worried

(*Softly*) Isn't she any better?
Philip There are times when I think she is, and then . . . It's awfully
difficult to tell . . .
Madge (*picking up the tray*) I wish you'd try and make her eat something.
Philip I've tried. It's no use. I can't even get her to take the sedative the
doctor left.
Madge Well, see if she'll have some coffee. Come along, Philip! It's worth
a try! She always says my coffee's better than anyone else's. (*As Philip
makes no attempt to take the tray from her*) All right, dear! It was just a
thought . . . (*She turns away*)
Philip Wait a minute! (*Relenting and taking the tray*) You could be right!
The coffee might be a good idea. We'll give it a try.

Philip exits to the bedroom

*Madge sighs, looks round the room, then more or less for something to do
starts straightening the cushions on the chairs. Finally she picks up her coat
and handbag from the sofa and moves towards the kitchen. The buzzer is
heard. Madge turns and looks towards the hall. The buzzer sounds again*

Madge puts down her things and goes into the hall. She returns accompanied by Lennox

Lennox How is your daughter-in-law? Is she any better?

Madge She's about the same, I think.

Lennox Has the doctor been?

Madge Yes, he called round last night, just after you left. He took forty minutes to tell us what we already knew—that she was suffering from shock!

Lennox Is Mr Harrison still here?

Madge Yes, he's with Stacey.

Lennox I'd very much like a word with him, if that's convenient.

Madge Yes, of course. (*She moves towards the bedroom, then hesitates*) Inspector, I know this must sound like an awfully stupid question, but—did Brad really commit suicide?

Lennox I don't think it's a stupid question, but if it is, it's one I've been asking myself ever since your son phoned me last night.

Madge Does that mean you're not sure? There's a doubt in your mind?

Lennox There's bound to be a doubt in my mind, Mrs Harrison, after the events of the past few days.

Philip enters. He looks a little less worried

Philip I thought I heard your voice, Inspector. Any news of Dominic?

Lennox No, I'm afraid not. We're still trying to locate him but we're not having much success at the moment. I'm sorry to hear Mrs Harrison doesn't feel any better, sir.

Philip Well, I think perhaps there is a slight improvement. (*To Madge*) You were right—but keep your fingers crossed—she's fallen for the coffee.

Madge There you are, you see! I told you! I'll try and cheer her up, Philip. (*She moves towards the bedroom*)

Philip Don't try too hard, Mother.

Madge exits to the bedroom

Lennox I saw Peter Lockwood this morning, sir. Amongst other things we discussed Charles Venner. Apparently Venner was a blackmailer—and by Lockwood's account a pretty clever one. However, when your wife arrived in Paris he made a mistake; an understandable one under the circumstances. He jumped to the conclusion that Mrs Harrison—like her father—was mixed up in the picture racket?

Philip Which is why, I imagine, he was keeping an eye on Stacey at the George Cinq?

Lennox Precisely—and why he followed her back to London. He intended to scare the hell out of her and then proceed to blackmail her father. Unfortunately for Venner things didn't turn out that way. (*Moving towards an armchair*) But this isn't what I came to see you about . . .

Philip Do sit down, Inspector.

Lennox Thank you, sir. (*He sits*) When I spoke to you last night about Brad Morris—about the conversation you'd had with him—you said, although he was obviously worried he most certainly didn't strike you as being suicidal.
Philip That's quite right. He didn't.
Lennox You stand by that statement?
Philip Yes, of course I do. Why do you ask?

Pause

Lennox It doesn't quite tie up with what Mr Kyle told me. We bumped into Mr Kyle last night, just as we were leaving here. He'd been having a skiing lesson.
Philip Yes, I know. (*Curiously*) What did Alan tell you exactly?
Lennox He said when your father-in-law returned from the hospital he was a very worried man. Extremely worried and very depressed. Mr Kyle said he was only with your father-in-law for about ten minutes but during that time Mr Morris talked about nothing but his health, his doctor, and the fact that he'd just been X-rayed.
Philip (*puzzled*) Alan—told you that?
Lennox Yes, sir. In fact he went further. He said he felt sure that's why Mr Morris had committed suicide.
Philip (*sceptically*) Because he was worried about his health?
Lennox Yes.
Philip I'm sorry, but I find that very difficult to believe. I spent at least ten minutes with Brad, not so very long after Alan saw him, and he never once mentioned his health or the fact that he'd been X-rayed.

Pause. Lennox looks at Philip again, quietly studying him

Lennox Well, apparently that wasn't Mr Kyle's experience. And let's face it, Mr Morris *was* ill. He *did* go to the hospital. He *did* have X-rays taken.
Philip Yes, I know. I'm aware of that.
Lennox And ten to one the Coroner will be made aware of it too, sir. And I can well imagine him being impressed by such information. Can't you?
Philip Yes, I can. I can indeed. But what about you, Inspector? Are you impressed by it, that's the point?

Pause. It is Philip who now studies the Inspector

Lennox There's no doubt in Mr Kyle's mind that your father-in-law was a very worried man. On the other hand, you saw him shortly after Mr Kyle did, and that wasn't your impression. So, accepting the fact that you are both telling the truth, there seems to be only one possible explanation.
Philip And what's that?
Lennox Mr Morris didn't want his daughter to know how he was really feeling, so he put on a bit of an act.
Philip You mean, he put on a bit of an act for my benefit?
Lennox Yes.
Philip But Alan Kyle sees a great deal more of my wife these days than I

do. They work together. So why didn't he put on an act for his benefit, as well as mine?

Lennox I—don't know, sir. I can't imagine why he didn't.

Lennox looks at Philip steadily. For a moment it appears as if he is about to make a comment, then he changes his mind and gets up

Thank you, Mr Harrison. When we pick up Dominic—and we will—I'll be in touch with you.

Lennox moves towards the hall followed by Philip

Madge comes out of the bedroom carrying the tray. Lennox exits

Philip turns and moves to Madge

Madge She still refuses to eat anything. But she's obviously enjoying the coffee.

Philip Good! We should have thought of it earlier.

Madge As a matter of fact—I hesitate to say it—but I think she's feeling better.

Philip looks at her

She's just told me to go home.

Philip (*delightedly*) Has she? That's a very good sign!

Madge She was nice about it. But I got the message.

Philip Yes, well I agree with Stacey. I think you ought to be making a move. You've been absolutely marvellous, as usual, but there's nothing else you can do for her, not at the moment at any rate.

Madge That's all very well, but what's going to happen? She can't be left on her own.

Philip (*quietly, yet with authority*) She's not going to be left on her own. I'm taking her back to the house where she'll be looked after.

Madge (*surprised*) Does she know that?

Philip No. Not yet. But I've made my mind up—and I'm not taking "no" for an answer.

Madge Then maybe I'd better be making a move!

Madge exits to the kitchen with the tray

Philip looks towards the bedroom then, deep in thought, moves to the sofa

Stacey enters. She is wearing a housecoat and shows obvious signs of distress. There is a tense look about her as she approaches Philip

Philip suddenly becomes aware of her

Philip Stacey!

Stacey Has Alan gone home?

Pause

Philip No; he's at Eaton Place. He's going home tonight.
Stacey Where's Madge?
Philip She's in the kitchen.
Stacey Is she angry with me?
Philip Angry? Good heavens, no!
Stacey I asked her . . . I told her to go home.
Philip Yes, I know.
Stacey I—I hope she wasn't annoyed, Philip?
Philip On the contrary. She was pleased. (*Smiling*) We both were. We took
    it as being a very good sign.
Stacey Your mother means well and I'm grateful to her. Please believe that.
    But I want to be left alone.
Philip I understand. I know how you feel.
Stacey Then be a darling and take Madge home. Please . . .
Philip Very well. But I'm afraid you're not going to get rid of me that easily.
    I shall come straight back, Stacey. There are several things I want to talk
    to you about.
Stacey What sort of things?
Philip We'll talk about them later.
Stacey (*tensely*) What sort of things?

A long pause

Philip As I understand it, Brad telephoned you last night, from the hospital?
Stacey Yes. I was at Eaton Place.
Philip Was he depressed at all?
Stacey (*after a moment*) No, I don't think so.
Philip Was he at all worried about himself, about what had happened at
    the hospital?
Stacey No. He sounded tired, but I wouldn't have said he was worried.
    Not unduly worried anyway. I don't know what you're thinking, but if
    Brad did commit suicide—and I'm not at all sure that he did—it certainly
    wasn't because of what happened yesterday at the hospital.

Philip gives a little nod

Madge enters

Philip picks up Madge's coat

Madge Ah—you're up, darling.
Philip I'm running you home, Mother.
Madge There's absolutely no need, I can easily pick up a cab.
Philip (*helping her with her coat*) I know you can, but you're not going to!
    The car's at the back, I'll bring it round to the front door. (*To Stacey*) I
    shan't be long.

Philip exits to the kitchen

Madge Are you sure you're going to be all right left on your own?

Stacey Yes, of course. I feel quite a bit better.

Madge looks at her, obviously not completely convinced

Honestly, darling.

Madge Well, if you want me you've only got to phone.

Stacey Yes, I know. You've been very sweet and I appreciate it.

Madge Nonsense! You just want to get rid of me!

Stacey Madge, it isn't that . . . (*Turning away from her; emotionally*) I just feel that—I'd like to be alone, for a little while at any rate.

Madge (*affectionately*) I know, my dear. I was only joking.

Stacey Philip says he's coming back. There's really no necessity for him to do so. Truly, Madge.

Tiny pause

Madge I think there is, Stacey. He wants to talk to you. (*Gently*) Please listen to what he's got to say. (*She kisses Stacey and picks up her handbag*)

Madge exits

Stacey follows Madge towards the hall, then turns and moves to the sofa. She stands for a moment preoccupied, thinking of Madge's remark. Voices are heard in the hall

Gerald (*off*) I'm Gerald Waddington. May I see Stacey?

Madge (*off*) I'm afraid she's not at all well. She's not seeing anyone at the moment.

Gerald (*off*) I'm afraid I must see her. It's most important.

Madge enters with an excited and somewhat bewildered looking Gerald. He has a newspaper under his arm and carries a valise

Madge (*faintly embarrassed*) It's Mr Waddington, Stacey . . .

Gerald Stace, my dear, I didn't know about Brad! (*Coming towards her*) I was at the airport and I suddenly saw a newspaper! I've never been so surprised—so shocked—in my life! (*Taking her arm*) My God, how awful for you!

Stacey It was very thoughtful of you to come, Gerald.

Gerald (*releasing her arm*) I had to come, Stace! I have to talk to you!

Stacey (*to Madge, with a reassuring little nod*) Thank you, Madge. (*As Madge hesitates*) It's all right, darling. There's no need to stay.

Madge looks at Gerald undecided whether to leave or not, then she finally accepts the situation and goes

Gerald Stace, I felt so desperately sorry for you. Are you all right, my dear?

Stacey I'm—I'm feeling a lot better than I did.

Gerald Mrs Harrison said you weren't well, that you were too ill to see anyone, but—I simply had to see you. (*Pause, hesitatingly*) I'm sure you don't want to talk about Brad, about what happened last night. But I've

got something to tell you. Something I think perhaps—you ought to
know . . .

Stacey (*surprised*) About Brad?

Gerald (*still a shade bewildered*) Well—yes, I—I suppose it's about Brad,
but I'm not really sure. I dropped in here last night in the hope of seeing
you but you were out and your father said I'd find you at Peter Lockwood's. I drove round to Eaton Place and then realized, of course, I
hadn't the slightest idea which house I was looking for. I tried to find
the address in the phone book but couldn't.

Stacey (*shaking her head*) Peter's ex-directory.

Gerald Yes, I suddenly realized that and so I telephoned Brad. At least—I
think it was Brad.

Stacey looks at him, obviously puzzled

Anyway, I dialled what I thought was this number and before I could
say anything a man's voice—which quite honestly I didn't recognize—
said, "Hold on—I'm in the kitchen. I've got some milk on the stove!"

*Stacey instinctively turns and looks at the table which previously held the
glass of milk*

I waited. I must have waited several minutes, then to my surprise I heard
music.

Stacey (*looking at Gerald again*) Music?

Gerald Yes. I was taken aback, I just couldn't understand it. Then after a
little while I heard a voice—a man's voice—somewhere in the back-
ground.

Stacey Was it Brad?

Gerald At the time I wasn't sure. But on reflection—I think it must have
been.

Stacey What did he say, can you remember?

Gerald He said something which sounded to me like: "I thought you were
having a lesson . . ."

Stacey (*softly, obviously surprised*) Having a lesson?

Gerald Yes.

Gerald looks at her, quietly surprised by both her expression and tone of voice

Stacey Are you sure that's what he said?

Gerald (*after a moment*) Yes, I'm pretty sure.

Pause

Stacey Go on, Gerald, What happened next?

Gerald Well—then I heard a noise. Like a bulb exploding. I realize now, of
course, that—it could have been a shot.

Stacey (*quietly*) Then what happened?

Gerald Nothing. A little while later I was cut off so I dialled again, making
absolutely sure that I dialled the right number. There was no reply.

Stacey (*after a moment*) Have you told anyone else about this?

Gerald No. Until I read in the paper about Brad, about what happened—

or what was supposed to have happened—it just didn't make sense. I'm not even sure that it makes sense now. I suppose I could have made a mistake and got the wrong number.

Stacey You say you heard music? What kind of music?

Gerald Oh dear . . .

Stacey moves to the record-player

Stacey Would you recognize the music if you heard it? (*She takes the record off the player and looks at it*)

Gerald Yes, I think perhaps I would.

Stacey replaces the record, switches on the set, and starts the player. Music. Pause. The music continues. Gerald moves slowly down to the record-player

Stacey Well?

Gerald (*listening to the music*) Yes! That's it! That's it, Stace!

Stacey stops the music

Stacey Thank you, Gerald. (*Thoughtfully*) You obviously didn't get the wrong number. It was Brad you spoke to.

Gerald Then I must have heard the shot.

Stacey Yes, darling, you must have done.

Stacey moves slowly away from the record-player. Gerald stands watching her. She is deep in thought. Pause.

Gerald (*softly*) What is it, Stace?

Another pause

Stacey Do you know a man who works for me called Alan Kyle?

Gerald Alan Kyle? Yes, I do. As a matter of fact he once tried to borrow some money from me.

Stacey Alan did?

Gerald Yes.

Stacey When was this?

Gerald Oh—about eighteen months ago. He said he was in trouble. Apparently he lost a lot of money on an antique shop or an art gallery. I'm not sure which.

Stacey It was an art gallery.

Gerald Yes, well—I didn't go into details because I hadn't the slightest intention of getting involved. (*Puzzled*) But why mention Alan Kyle?

Stacey (*softly*) He's been staying here, while I've been away.

Gerald With—Brad?

Stacey (*almost as if to herself*) Yes, with Brad. (*A long, thoughtful pause, then she reaches a decision*) Gerald, please excuse me, I want to make a phone call.

She goes to the phone and dials a number. Gerald stands watching her. There is a pause

(*On the phone*) . . . This is Stacey Harrison, I'd like to speak to Mr

Kyle . . . (*Pause*) Alan—it's Stacey. (*Tiny pause*) Yes . . . I am a little
better. (*Softly*) Alan, I want to talk to you about something . . . I can't,
not now, there's someone with me . . . Yes, it is, it's very important
. . . (*Slight hesitation*) No, it's about . . . Brad. (*Pause*) Well, could
you drop in this evening sometime, on your way home? (*Pause*) Thank
you, Alan. I'll see you then . . .

*Gerald, obviously puzzled, is still watching Stacey as she slowly replaces the
receiver, and—*

the Lights fade to a Black-out

SCENE 3

The same. Saturday night

*The room looks the same except that one of the tables has been moved slightly
nearer the sofa. There is a large bowl of flowers on this table and next to it
stands an open box of Kleenex tissues*

*For a brief moment the room is deserted then Stacey enters from the kitchen
wearing a housecoat and carrying a glass of milk. She looks serious and is
obviously embarked on a course of action. She puts the glass down on one of
the other tables (the table previously used by Brad for the milk), looks round
the room, turns off the main lights then crosses and switches on the record-
player. Music. It is the record we have heard previously. Ravel's La Valse
Rhapsodie Espagnole. Stacey stands for a moment adjusting the volume, then
she moves across to the telephone and picks up the receiver. She makes no
attempt to dial a number but simply puts the receiver down on the writing
table. Having done this she opens a drawer in the table and takes out a small
revolver. She carefully examines this gun, first releasing the safety catch, then
opening and closing the chamber, finally sighting her eyes along the barrel.
Apparently satisfied with the weapon she puts it into the pocket of her housecoat. She now surveys the dimly lit room, her eyes finally coming to rest on the
bowl of flowers*

*The door buzzer sounds. Stacey freezes and looks towards the hall. Pause.
Buzzer sounds again. Stacey does not move; she is still looking towards the
hall when the buzzer is heard yet again. Long pause. A noise is heard in the
hall. Stacey quickly goes into the bedroom. Another pause*

*Alan enters, carrying his overcoat. He is obviously a little taken aback to find
the room empty and the music playing. As he moves slowly into the room his
expression changes from one of surprise to faint bewilderment. He stands
looking at the record-player, then as he puts down his coat he sees the glass
of milk. Puzzled, he moves in the direction of the dining room, staring at the
glass of milk—then a sudden thought occurs to him and he whips round and
looks at the telephone. He sees that it is "off the hook". He stands bewildered,
staring in turn at the telephone, the glass of milk and the record-player. Pause.
Music continues*

Suddenly, with almost a touch of panic in his movements, Alan turns back towards the hall. At this moment Stacey appears from the bedroom. She is still wearing the housecoat, but somehow looks different. There is a strange, almost far away look about her as she stares at Alan

Stacey Alan—how long have you been here?
Alan I've just arrived.
Stacey What time is it?
Alan It's—it's about eight o'clock.
Stacey Eight o'clock?
Alan Yes . . .

Pause

Stacey (*dazed*) I'm sorry, I must have fallen asleep. (*Indicating the record-player*) Do you mind—turning that off . . .?

Alan hesitates, his eyes still on Stacey, then he crosses and switches off the record. Another pause

Alan Aren't you feeling well?
Stacey I felt so much better about an hour ago. I felt better than I've been feeling all day. Then suddenly—while I was getting myself a glass of milk—I felt terribly faint. In the end—I had to go back to bed.
Alan I see. (*Pause*) Why is the phone like that?
Stacey Phone?
Alan It's off the hook.
Stacey Oh. Have you been trying to get through then?
Alan No, I just wondered why—it was like that . . .
Stacey So many people have been phoning about Brad, I couldn't stand it any longer.
Alan (*almost relieved by her explanation*) Oh. Oh, I see.
Stacey I think I'd like a drink, Alan. Would you mind getting me one?
Alan Yes, of course.

Alan moves to the drinks trolley. Stacey moves towards the sofa, pausing for a moment by the table with the bowl of flowers on it. As she does so she glances across at Alan who is now standing with his back to her. Satisfied that he can't see what she is doing, she puts her hand inside the Kleenex box. It is obvious from her movements that there is something inside the box. Alan turns, glass in hand, and just for a flicker of a second Stacey is taken by surprise, then she casually takes a tissue out of the box and continues down to the sofa

(*unaware of anything unusual*) Would you like some soda with this?
Stacey No, I don't think so. (*She sits on the sofa*) Please help yourself, Alan. (*Tiny pause*) How did you get on today?
Alan Very well, considering. If we can get the carpet people to play ball we should be finished by the end of the week. (*Moving down to the sofa*) Here we are, Stacey.
Stacey Aren't you having one?

Alan No, I don't think I'll chance it. I've got to drive out to Dedham later tonight. Oh, before I forget. Here's your door key. (*He puts the key on the table*)

Pause. Stacey sips her drink. Alan joins her on the sofa. Another pause

Alan Do you feel any better?

Stacey I still feel—a little odd.

Alan (*after a moment*) Are you on your own?

Stacey Yes. Madge offered to stay with me, but—well, you know Madge.

Alan Where's Philip?

Stacey I don't know. He was here earlier. I imagine he's gone back to the house.

Pause

Alan You said you wanted to see me. About Brad . . .

Stacey (*looking at him*) About Brad?

Alan (*lightly*) Yes. That's what you said. You telephoned me.

Stacey Yes, that's right. I did! I wanted to ask you something. (*Leaning towards him*) While I was away, while you were staying here, did Brad have many visitors?

Alan Visitors? You mean—people dropping in for a drink, that sort of thing?

Stacey Yes.

Alan I don't think so. Of course I was at Peter's, working most of the time. Certainly during the day. But why do you ask?

Stacey I wondered if, by any chance, there was one particular person. Someone Brad saw a great deal of.

Alan I can't remember anyone, off hand. (*Thoughtfully*) He went out to Kingsford once or twice to see some of his old cronies but so far as I know he never invited any of them back here.

Stacey (*apparently disappointed*) I see.

Alan Stacey—I'm sorry—maybe I'm a little dense—but I don't get the point of all this.

Pause

Stacey Alan, I know you won't agree with me, but—I don't think Brad did commit suicide.

Alan (*softly, apparently desperately sorry for her*) Oh, Stacey!

Stacey In fact, I know he didn't!

Alan Then what do you think happened?

Stacey (*looking at him, tensely*) I know what happened!

Alan (*gently*) All right, if you know what happened, tell me . . .

Stacey He was murdered!

Alan (*shaking his head*) Now I ask you, who on earth would want to murder poor old Brad? Stacey, please listen to me. I saw Brad last night. I had a long talk to him. I didn't tell you everything he said because at the time I didn't want to upset you. But believe me—and you must believe me, for your own peace of mind—your father really was a *very* worried man.

Stacey I'm sorry, I don't believe that. And even if you're telling me the truth—

Alan (*slightly surprised by the remark*) I am telling you the truth!

Stacey —Brad would never, never have committed suicide!

Alan Stacey, how do you know that? How can you be sure of a thing like that? You don't know how Brad felt. What his feelings were, his true feelings, when he returned from the hospital.

Stacey No, I don't. But there's something you don't know, too, Alan. (*Rising*) Something I haven't told you, something I haven't told anyone . . . (*She moves away from the sofa, putting down her drink. After a brief silence she turns and looks at him*)

Stacey I spoke to Brad last night, just before—he was shot. I heard everything, Alan. Everything that happened.

Alan What do you mean—you heard everything? (*He rises and faces her*)

Stacey I was on the phone. Brad spoke to me. He said . . .

Alan Wait a minute! Start at the beginning. Where were you? Where did you phone from?

Stacey From a phone near the Clinic. I'd gone to see Peter Lockwood. When I arrived there I suddenly remembered something I wanted to talk to Brad about . . .

Alan (*moving nearer her*) Go on . . .

Stacey It was some little time before Brad came to the phone. He was in the kitchen. When he did answer it he told me to hang on. I waited. I must have waited several minutes and then suddenly, to my surprise, I heard music.

Alan moves a shade nearer her

Alan Music?

Stacey Yes. From the record-player.

Alan How do you know it was from the record-player?

Stacey I recognized the music. It was the Ravel record you gave Brad for his birthday.

Alan moves another step nearer Stacey. She does not move

Alan Then what happened?

Stacey Then I heard Brad talking to someone. I heard him say: "I thought you were having a lesson."

Alan "I thought you were having a lesson?"

Stacey Yes.

Pause

Alan (*very near her*) Are you sure he said that?

Stacey (*watching him, not moving, but her hand now in the pocket of her housecoat*) Yes, I'm quite sure.

Alan Did you hear any other voices?

Stacey No, I didn't.

Alan But you're sure that's what Brad said: "I thought you were having a lesson?"
Stacey (*tensely, a shade frightened*) Yes.

Pause

Alan And you haven't told anyone else about this?
Stacey No, I haven't.
Alan Not even Philip?
Stacey No-one.
Alan And you're—sure about this?
Stacey Yes, I'm quite sure.

Alan stares at her and she now backs slowly away from him, her hand in her pocket, on the gun. It is obvious that she is tensed up, waiting for the moment when he will give himself away by attacking her. But to Stacey's surprise, Alan does not do this. Instead he makes a little gesture of incomprehension and turns away

Alan Stacey, you're incredible! Don't you realize this information could be important! Why on earth haven't you told the police about this?
Stacey (*puzzled and surprised by Alan's reaction; thinking fast*) I—I was so distressed. So upset by what had happened, I just didn't stop to think.
Alan All right. Fair enough. But why send for me? Why tell me about it? Why not Philip?
Stacey I thought perhaps you might be able to—identify him . . .
Alan You mean, the person Brad was talking to?
Stacey Yes.
Alan But why should I be able to identify him? And how do you know it was a man? You say you only heard one voice—Brad's?
Stacey Yes.
Alan Then for all you know, it could have been a woman he was talking to?
Stacey Yes. Yes, I—suppose it could have been.
Alan After all, if it was an ex-pupil of Brad's, it could very easily have been a woman.
Stacey An ex-pupil?
Alan Yes.
Stacey Why—an ex-pupil?
Alan Well, surely it must have been someone from Kingsford, from the Art School? Otherwise, what was all that about a lesson?

Stacey is somewhat stunned by this statement of Alan's. It is obvious that the possibility of an art lesson had never occurred to her. Slight pause

Alan Is something the matter? Don't you feel well? (*Silence*) What is it, Stacey?
Stacey (*reflecting on what he has said*) Nothing. Nothing. Alan.

He continues looking at her, apparently concerned

Alan Are you sure? Do you feel faint or something?

Stacey No. No, I'm perfectly all right. It was just that . . . (*Recovering her composure*) I'm sorry about tonight. Dragging you back here like this, just when you were on your way home. It was stupid of me. You're perfectly right, of course. I should have consulted Philip, not you.

Alan (*indicating the phone*) You can still consult him, if you want to. Although, the way you're feeling at the moment, I think you'd be well advised to sleep on it. (*Going to his coat*) In fact, if I were you I wouldn't talk to anyone. Certainly not tonight. I'd leave the phone off the hook and go straight to bed.

Stacey That's certainly what I feel like.

Alan Then I should do it. Have you any sleeping pills?

Stacey Yes, I have.

Alan How many do you usually take?

Stacey Oh—just one every now and again, when I feel like it.

Alan Then I should take two and make sure of a good night's sleep. (*Picking up his things*) I might be a little late tomorrow morning. Depends on the traffic. Also, with being away, there's one or two things I'd like to do at the cottage.

Stacey Yes, of course. Please yourself when you get to Peter's. And thank you for coming.

Alan Try and get some sleep, Stacey.

Alan exits

As we hear the closing of the front door Stacey turns towards the bedroom, then hesitates. She stands perfectly still, obviously thinking, trying to reach a decision about something. Pause. Then she turns away from the bedroom and crosses to the writing table. She replaces the telephone receiver, lifts it, and starts to dial. But her thoughts appear to be elsewhere and half-way through the dialling she hesitates, not sure whether to continue dialling or not. Finally she changes her mind about the call and, replacing the receiver, goes to the sofa. Pause. She still has a preoccupied, somewhat dazed look about her as she sits on the sofa turning over in her mind her interview with Alan. She takes the gun out of her pocket and stares at it. It is difficult to tell precisely what she is thinking. The telephone rings. For a little while she appears to be unaware of it, and makes no movement. As it continues to ring she puts the gun down on the sofa so that it is partly concealed by a cushion, then rises and goes to the writing-table

Alan enters from the hall as Stacey reaches the table. He has got rid of his coat, but now has a scarf hanging loosely around his shoulders

Stacey stares at him in amazement, her hand on the phone

Alan Don't answer it!

Alan moves towards her, pulling the scarf from his shoulders as he does so. Stacey slowly backs away from the table, frightened not only by the tone of his voice but by the expression on his face. As he watches her he holds the

scarf between both hands, twisting it around, making it taut, ready for action.
It is obvious that he intends to strangle her with it. The phone stops ringing

Stacey What are you going to do?
Alan It's a pity you made that phone call, Stacey.

Pause

Stacey (*attempting to hide her fear*) Phone call . . .
Alan Last night, to Brad. But I'm glad you didn't tell anyone else about it.
Most thoughtful of you. But as it happens, not very sensible.

Another pause

Stacey (*quietly*) I didn't make the call.

Alan freezes; stares at her

Alan What do you mean—you didn't make it?
Stacey Just that. I didn't make it. A friend of mine made the call.
Alan You're lying!
Stacey All right. I'm lying.

Short pause

Alan Who was it? Who was this friend?
Stacey It's—not important.
Alan It is to me! Who was it?

A tense silence. Alan, obviously rattled, continues staring at her

Stacey (*softly, yet with almost a suggestion of defiance*) You're not sure, are
you Alan? You're just not sure. You don't know whether I'm telling you
the truth or not!
Alan (*flaring up*) No, I don't! But I'll bloody soon find out!

He throws the scarf down and, picking up a bottle from the nearby drinks
trolley, deliberately smashes it against the side of the trolley. He now faces
Stacey with the jagged edge of the broken bottle (See note on p. 74)

(*intensely angry, threatening her*) Now tell me the truth! Who made that
call?

Pause

Stacey I've told you! I told you who made it! A friend of mine.

Stacey makes a sudden movement in the direction of the hall but Alan
forestalls her

Alan (*viciously*) You stupid bitch!

As she shrinks back from him, now obviously terrified, he moves nearer to her,
gradually forcing her towards the bedroom

Get into the bedroom!

She shakes her head and backs away from him

Do as I tell you, get in there!

He moves closer. Stacey is desperate, her eyes fixed on the broken bottle. She now realizes that her only hope of survival is to reach the sofa and get possession of the gun. She is backing further away from him and is within a few feet of the bedroom when she makes what Alan mistakenly believes to be a last desperate attempt to reach the hall. He immediately falls back, his body blocking any possible escape. This movement is precisely what Stacey hoped for, and she literally throws herself in the opposite direction, towards the sofa. Alan is astonished; it is several seconds before he recovers. Then with a look of intense anger on his face he moves down to where she is now standing. He stops dead in his tracks; thunderstruck; staring at the revolver which is now in Stacey's shaking hand

Where the hell did that come from?

Pause. Stacey's hand gradually stops shaking and she very slowly, very determinedly, moves round the sofa, drawing nearer to him. Alan hesitates, then realizing that she means business, drops the bottle

Stacey (*softly*) Why did you murder my father?
Alan I—I didn't murder him! I swear to you I didn't!
Stacey Tell me about it!
Alan I—I didn't murder Brad, Stacey! Honestly I didn't! I'll tell you precisely what took place if you'll . . . (*Retreating*) Now, please, don't be a damn fool, put that away!
Stacey Tell me, Alan!
Alan (*in an attempt to play it cool*) Look, Stacey, if you put that gun down I'll tell you exactly what happened . . .
Stacey (*suddenly angry, unable to keep a note of hysteria out of her voice*) Tell me now! You bastard!
Alan (*slowly, obviously very scared, his eyes on the gun*) I was frightened that Brad might talk and make it impossible for Dominic and me to go on working together. We'd already scared the life out of Peter so we decided to—try and do the same to Brad. Unfortunately, the moment Brad saw me . . .

Alan is interrupted by the loud shrieking of police sirens. Both Alan and Stacey are startled—taken completely by surprise—and they instinctively turn towards the window. There is a brief hiatus—then Alan taken immediate advantage of the situation. He lunges towards Stacey and with a vicious blow knocks the revolver out of her hand. As he turns to make a quick getaway she makes a desperate attempt to grab hold of him at the same time screaming for help

Alan Leave go! (*As she grimly holds on to him*) Leave go! Let go of me!

The police sirens are followed by the screeching of car brakes and the banging of car doors

(*Frenziedly*) You bitch!

Stacey frantically tries to hold him, but he finally manages to release himself and shoving her violently aside races out into the hall

   Alan exits

We hear the opening of the front door and then the sound of a wild struggle and excited voices. Stacey is exhausted and desperately near to tears as she sinks on to the sofa, finally burying her head in her hands. Long pause. From the street we hear the sound of voices. Car doors. Police sirens

   Philip enters and quietly moves to the sofa. He stands by Stacey, staring down at her

After a little while Stacey becomes aware of Philip's presence and slowly raises her head

Philip (*gently, but with a serious undertone*) Did he hurt you?
Stacey No. No, I'm all right.
Philip Are you sure?

Stacey gives a little nod and as she does so Philip notices the gun on the floor near the sofa. He picks it up

Philip Is this yours?
Stacey Yes . . .
Philip Is it loaded?
Stacey Yes.

Philip looks at her

Yes, it is! And I was going to kill him! I wanted to kill him!

Philip makes no comment, but stares at the revolver, obviously concerned

Why did you come? How did you know about Alan?
Philip (*still looking at the gun*) Gerald telephoned me. He was worried. He knew you were up to something but he didn't know what it was. I'm afraid he doesn't know you as well as I do, Stacey.

There is a sudden noise from the hall and Philip quickly makes a decision: he unloads the gun and slips the cartridges into his pocket

   Lennox enters. The Inspector appears somewhat determined, but his manner is not unfriendly

Lennox Well—Mrs Harrison! I'm glad to see that you're all right! But by God, I'm not at all sure that you deserve to be!

Lennox sees the gun in Philip's hand

Philip (*casually*) You'd better take care of this. It's my wife's. It's not loaded. She was merely trying to frighten him with it.

Stacey rises. Lennox examines the gun, then turns towards Stacey

Lennox Strictly off the record, Mrs Harrison—and speaking as a bachelor —there are many things I admire about you. But you really shouldn't try and take the law into your own hands.

Stacey I'm sorry, Inspector.

Lennox If Gerald Waddington hadn't telephoned your husband and your husband hadn't had the good sense to telephone me I shudder to think what might have happened to you. (*Drily, looking at the gun*) Or to Mr Kyle for that matter. (*He puts the gun in his pocket*) Now I suggest you tell me exactly what happened this evening.

Stacey (*weakly*) Oh, dear! Must I, Inspector? I really don't know where . . .

Philip (*coming to her rescue*) Inspector, I appreciate that my wife will have to make a statement, but under the circumstances—and speaking as a married man—could I bring her down to the station in about twenty minutes?

Lennox hesitates

Lennox (*after a moment*) Yes, all right, sir. I'll expect you both in about twenty minutes.

Lennox exits

Pause

Philip Would you like a drink?

Stacey No. No, I don't think so. But please help yourself, Philip, I'm sure you can do with one.

Philip shakes his head. He stands looking at her. Pause

What will happen at the police station?

Philip You'll have to make a statement and they'll question you about the gun. But there's nothing for you to worry about. I'll tell you what to say later.

Stacey Thank you. (*Softly*) I always seem to be saying that to you these days, don't I? (*She moves to the box of tissues on the table*) I suppose in view of what's happened, I'd better let the Inspector take care of this. (*She removes the box of tissues and reveals a portable tape recorder*)

Philip stares at the tape recorder in astonishment

Philip What on earth is that doing here?

Stacey It's a tape recorder.

Philip Yes, I can see what it is! But what's it doing here?

Stacey Can't you guess? (*Facing him, defiantly*) I knew you wouldn't believe me if I told you about Alan—so I decided to record what happened! (*Relenting slightly, and turning away*) Anyway, I doubt very much whether it's been working properly. I'm not mechanically minded, I'm afraid.

Philip (*with a smile, moving to her*) You have other attributes, Stacey.

CURTAIN

FURNITURE AND PROPERTY LIST

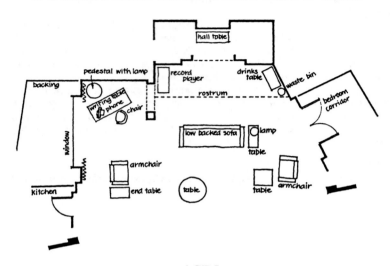

ACT I

SCENE 1

On stage: Sofa. *On it:* cushions, assorted presents including LP record, several
bottles of after-shave lotion, art books, birthday cards
Sofa table. *On it:* more presents as above, lamp, antique silver cigarette
box, lighter, ashtray
2 armchairs
3 occasional tables. *On them:* ashtrays
Small chair at writing table
Pedestal with lamp
Hall table
Record-player and records
Drinks trolley or table. *On it:* gin, Scotch, sherry, tonic water, soda
syphon, glasses, knife, bottle-opener. *Beside it:* waste-bin
Writing-table. *On it:* telephone, note pad, writing materials, several
unopened letters, paper-knife, dressing
On walls: several pictures
Carpet
Window curtains to ground
Off stage: Carrier bag (**Madge**)
Wrapped bottle of after-shave lotion (**Madge**)
Briefcase and evening paper (**Alan**)
Zipped travelling bag (**Stacey**)
Suitcase, several pairs of shoes, cardigan, picture in linen sack with
cord (**Alan**)
Bathrobe and turban (**Stacey**)
Housecoat (**Stacey**)
Telegram (**Stacey**)

Personal: **Alan:** door key, leather wrist-strap
         Stacey: car key

SCENE 2

Strike: Presents
         Alan's briefcase and paper
         Used glasses
Set: LP record by record-player
         Tray with coffee cup, saucer, spoon (used), coffee-pot, cream jug, sugar
           bowl, on table by sofa
         Morning newspapers on sofa
Off stage: Briefcase containing diary and photograph (**Lennox**)

SCENE 3

Strike: Newspapers
         Coffee tray
Set: Collection of fabrics and curtain materials, and several account books,
           on writing table.
Off stage: Overnight case (**Stacey**)
         Passport (**Alan**)
Personal: **Alan:** watch
         Stacey: car key

ACT II

SCENE 1

Strike: Fabrics and account books from writing table
         Used glasses
Set: Roll of curtain material in hall
         Open telegram in writing table drawer
         Unopened bottle of Scotch on drinks trolley
Off stage: LP record (**Alan**)
         Dressing-gown (**Alan**)
         Linen picture sack fastened with wire and containing Dufy-style paint-
           ing (**Stacey**)
         Biscuit (**Brad**)
         Ski Jacket (**Alan**)
         Gloves (**Alan**)
         Glass of hot milk (**Brad**)
Personal: **Gerald:** watch
         Brad: watch

SCENE 2

Strike: Curtain material
         Painting and sack
         Glass of milk
Set: Alan's case and valise on floor
         Madge's coat and handbag on sofa
Off stage: Tray with cup, saucer, spoon, coffee-pot, cream jug, sugar bowl, plate
           of sandwiches (**Madge**)
         Valise and newspaper (**Gerald**)

SCENE 3

Set: Occasional table close to sofa. *On it:* large bowl of flowers, open box
             of Kleenex tissues with small tape-recorder concealed inside
             Small revolver in writing table drawer
             Trick breakable bottle on drinks trolley*
Off stage: Glass of milk (Stacey)
             *A ski stick can be substituted for the broken bottle. Alan will then
             enter from the hall, ski stick in hand, as Stacey reaches the table.

LIGHTING PLOT

Property fittings required: wall brackets, 2 table lamps
INTERIOR. A living-room. The same scene throughout

ACT I SCENE 1 Evening
To open: All brackets on, table lamps off
Cue 1:   Stacey turns on one table lamp   (Page 11)
              Snap on first lamp and covering spots
Cue 2:   Stacey turns off main lights   (Page 11)
              Snap off wall brackets
Cue 3:   Stacey turns on one table lamp   (Page 11)
              Snap on second lamp and covering spots
Cue 4:   Philip nods   (Page 15)
              Fade to Black-out

ACT I SCENE 2 Morning
To open: General daylight effect
Cue 5:   Stacey gives Philip a long look   (Page 22)
              Fade to Black-out

ACT I SCENE 3 Morning
To open: As Scene 2
No cues

ACT II SCENE 1 Evening
To open: Brackets and table lamp on
Cue 6:   After Alan's exit   (Page 53)
              Fade to Black-out

ACT II SCENE 2 Morning
To open: As Act 1 Scene 2
Cue 7:   Stacey replaces telephone receiver   (Page 62)
              Fade to Black-out

ACT II SCENE 3 Night
To open: Brackets and all table lamps on
Cue 8:   Stacey turns off main lights   (Page 62)
              Snap off all brackets

EFFECTS PLOT

ACT I

Scene 1

Cue 1:	**Brad** opens bottle of after-shave lotion	(Page 1)
	Front door buzzer sounds	
Cue 2:	**Stacey** exits to bedroom	(Page 11)
	Pause, then sound of running bath-water	
Cue 3:	Immediately following Cue 2	(Page 11)
	Telephone rings	
Cue 4:	Shortly after Cue 3	(Page 11)
	Door buzzer sounds several times	
Cue 5:	**Stacey** moves to phone	(Page 11)
	Telephone stops ringing	
Cue 6:	**Stacey** exits to bedroom	(Page 11)
	Pause, then bath-water effect off	
Cue 7:	**Venner** picks up silver box	(Page 14)
	Door buzzer sounds—twice	
Cue 8:	**Stacey** replaces telephone receiver	(Page 15)
	Door buzzer sounds—twice	

Scene 2

Cue 9:	**Brad:** ". . . by the look of things!"	(Page 16)
	Telephone rings	
Cue 10:	**Philip:** "But it's not important."	(Page 18)
	Door buzzer sounds	

Scene 3

Cue 11:	Shortly after Curtain rises	(Page 23)
	Door buzzer sounds	
Cue 12:	**Gerald:** "Super."	(Page 27)
	Door buzzer sounds	
Cue 13:	**Stacey:** ". . . so you don't believe it!"	(Page 29)
	Pause, then door buzzer sounds	
Cue 14:	**Stacey** nods	(Page 29)
	Door buzzer sounds	

ACT II

Scene 1

Cue 15:	**Alan** exits to bedroom	(Page 37)
	Door buzzer sounds	
Cue 16:	**Alan** moves to record-player	(Page 37)
	Door buzzer sounds—twice	
Cue 17:	**Brad:** ". . . pretty little blonde."	(Page 37)
	Door buzzer sounds	
Cue 18:	**Brad** nods	(Page 39)
	Telephone rings	
Cue 19:	**Alan** exits	(Page 40)
	Telephone rings	

76 The Gentle Hook

MADE AND PRINTED IN GREAT BRITAIN BY
LATIMER TREND & COMPANY LTD, PLYMOUTH
MADE IN ENGLAND

Lightning Source UK Ltd.
Milton Keynes UK
UKOW01f1401310715

256163UK00014B/193/P